HTML5 Web Application Development By Example Beginner's guide

Learn how to build rich, interactive web applications from the ground up using HTML5, CSS3, and jQuery

J.M. Gustafson

BIRMINGHAM - MUMBAI

HTML5 Web Application Development By Example
Beginner's guide

First published: June 2013

Production Reference: 1170613

Published by Packt Publishing Ltd.
Livery Place
35 Livery Street
Birmingham B3 2PB, UK.

ISBN 978-1-84969-594-7

www.packtpub.com

Cover Image by Faiz Fattohi (faizfattohi@gmail.com)

Credits

Author
J.M. Gustafson

Reviewers
Chad Adams
Dale Cruse

Acquisition Editor
Martin Bell

Lead Technical Editor
Anila Vincent

Technical Editors
Dominic Pereira
Madhuri Das
Kirti Pujari
Joyslita D'souza
Veronica Fernandes

Project Coordinator
Rahul Dixit

Proofreader
Samantha Lyon

Indexer
Hemangini Bari

Graphics
Ronak Dhruv

Production Coordinator
Melwyn D'sa

Cover Work
Melwyn D'sa

About the Author

J.M. Gustafson is a professional software engineer who started programming on a VIC-20 in the 80s and hasn't stopped since. He has a degree in Computer Science and has been working with web technologies writing enterprise applications for nearly his entire career. Currently, he spends most of his time writing web apps and services in C# and JavaScript.

In his free time he enjoys spending time with his family, playing music, writing, and the outdoors. When he's not doing any of that, you can find him doing (what else?) more programming. These days he is particularly interested in writing games using HTML5 and JavaScript, many of which you can find on his website at `WorldTreeSoftware.com`.

I would like to thank my good friends Pat Calahan and Thomas Fonseca for reviewing my chapters and giving me great feedback and encouragement. Thanks to my family for giving me the time to spend writing this book. Thanks also to the editors at Packt for giving me the opportunity to write this book and guiding me along the path to publication.

About the Reviewer

Dale Cruse is the author of *HTML5 Multimedia Development Cookbook* (*Packt Publishing*) and a technical editor of several other HTML5 books. He started his career in 1995 as a U.S. Army photojournalist. Since switching to purely digital at `CBSNews.com`, he's created web and mobile experiences for some of the most well known clients in the world, including 20th Century Fox, Bloomingdale's, and MINI Cooper. Currently, he juggles being both a senior developer at Allen & Gerritsen and being a New York Yankees fan in South Boston. An in-demand speaker, you can't get him to shut up on Twitter at `@dalecruse`.

www.PacktPub.com

Support files, eBooks, discount offers and more

You might want to visit www.PacktPub.com for support files and downloads related to your book.

Did you know that Packt offers eBook versions of every book published, with PDF and ePub files available? You can upgrade to the eBook version at www.PacktPub.com and as a print book customer, you are entitled to a discount on the eBook copy. Get in touch with us at service@packtpub.com for more details.

At www.PacktPub.com, you can also read a collection of free technical articles, sign up for a range of free newsletters and receive exclusive discounts and offers on Packt books and eBooks.

http://PacktLib.PacktPub.com

Do you need instant solutions to your IT questions? PacktLib is Packt's online digital book library. Here, you can access, read and search across Packt's entire library of books.

Why Subscribe?

- ◆ Fully searchable across every book published by Packt
- ◆ Copy and paste, print and bookmark content
- ◆ On demand and accessible via web browser

Free Access for Packt account holders

If you have an account with Packt at www.PacktPub.com, you can use this to access PacktLib today and view nine entirely free books. Simply use your login credentials for immediate access.

Table of Contents

Preface

The time to start using HTML5 is now. HTML5 provides a complete application development framework for writing full featured applications that run in the web browser. Even though the HTML5 specification hasn't been fully completed yet, the most popular features are already widely supported by nearly every modern browser running on devices, from desktops to tablets to smartphones. That means you can write an application once and have it run on nearly any device.

If you are looking to start writing HTML5 web applications but don't know where to start, then this book is for you. We will start with the basics of building a web application and then learn about HTML5, CSS3, and JavaScript by building real working applications. This is not a reference book. We will keep the theory to a minimum and hands-on coding to a maximum.

Just a few years ago, writing full-featured applications in the browser required other technologies such as Flash or Java Applets that ran as browser plugins. Like most people, I had only used JavaScript to write simple client validation scripts. I didn't even think it was possible to write real applications using JavaScript. That all started to change when a couple of things happened.

Firstly, I discovered jQuery. Here was a library that made writing JavaScript a whole lot easier by abstracting away browser idiosyncrasies and making it very easy to manipulate the elements of a web page. Plus it could help us perform some cool actions, such as animating elements. Then about three years ago I found out about HTML5 while looking for a way to draw graphics primitives directly onto a web page. Since then I've watched HTML5 develop into a complete framework, capable of being used to write real applications without plugins.

This book is the culmination of those past three years of writing JavaScript nearly every day, learning what works and what doesn't. A technical brain dump, if you will. The objective was to write the book that I would have liked to read when I started out.

The future of HTML5 web application development looks bright. All of the big hitters in the world of web browser development are putting their full support behind HTML5 and JavaScript. HTML5 is the future of web application development!

What this book covers

Chapter 1, *The Task at Hand*, will teach you the basic components of a JavaScript application by building a template that can be used to start writing new applications. Then we will create a tasklist application where we will learn how to manipulate the DOM and how to use HTML5 Web Storage to save the state of the application.

Chapter 2, *Let's Get Stylish*, will show how to use the new CSS3 features to add professional-looking styles to your web applications including rounded corners, shadows, and gradients. We will also learn how to use CSS sprites to make loading images more efficient.

Chapter 3, *The Devil is in the Details*, will teach you about the new HTML5 form input types by adding a details section to the tasklist application. We will also learn about custom data attributes and learn how to use them to bind data in the view to the model.

Chapter 4, *A Blank Canvas*, will show how to use the new Canvas element and API to draw directly onto a web page by creating a drawing application. We will also learn how to handle touch events from touch-screen devices.

Chapter 5, *Not So Blank Canvas*, will continue teaching about the canvas by showing you how to export images from a canvas and load images into a canvas using the new File API. Then we will get down to the pixel level and learn how to directly manipulate canvas image data.

Chapter 6, *Piano Man*, will teach you how to use the Audio element and API to play sounds in a web page. We will create a virtual piano that plays sounds when the keys are clicked.

Chapter 7, *Piano Hero*, will take the virtual piano from the previous chapter and turn it into a game where the player must play the correct notes of a song at the correct time to get points. In the process we will learn about using JavaScript timers and animating elements.

Chapter 8, *A Change in the Weather*, will show you how to get data from servers and talk to web services using Ajax. We will build a weather widget that gets the user's location using the Geolocation API and displays their local weather report with data from a web service.

Chapter 9, *Web Workers Unite*, will teach you how to use HTML5 web workers to perform long running processes in a separate thread to make your applications more responsive. We will create an application that draws Mandelbrot fractals onto a canvas using a web worker.

Chapter 10, *Releasing an App into the Wild*, will teach you how to use a JavaScript compressor to combine and compress your application's JavaScript files before releasing it to the world. We will also learn how to create applications that can be used offline by using the HTML5 Application Cache.

What you need for this book

The great thing about HTML5 is that there is no cost to use it. You don't need any special tools or licenses to develop web applications. However, using a good code editor will help you a lot, especially as you get started. There's nothing like autosuggest to help you remember JavaScript functions, element names, and styling options. And syntax highlighting is essential for making it easier to read code.

That said, there are a few source code editors that I can suggest if you don't already have one. Notepad++ is a free editor with JavaScript, HTML, and CSS syntax highlighting and some basic autosuggest, without a lot of overhead. I used it to write all of the code in this book. On the higher end, Microsoft Visual Studio provides very good autosuggest features but with more overhead than a basic text editor. Another great option is NetBeans, an open source IDE written in Java with good web development support.

You will also need a web browser with good HTML5 support and developer tools. The latest versions of most browsers support the HTML5 features used in this book. The browser you use should depend on which has the developer tools you like most. I use Chrome because it has great developer tools built-in. Firefox with the Firebug plugin installed is also very good. For this book I use Chrome as the browser of choice. Internet Explorer 9 doesn't completely support all of the HTML5 features we will be learning and the developer tools are not as good as the others, so I would stay away from using it for development.

The one other thing you may need is a web server such as IIS or Apache. Most of the time you can open your web application right from the filesystem when in development. However, some HTML5 features will only work through a web server. I have noted the places in this book where that is the case.

Who this book is for

This book is for the programmer who has experience in other languages and wants to start writing HTML5 web applications. You should have some basic knowledge of HTML, CSS, and JavaScript. For example, you should know how to write simple HTML documents. You should also know the basics of using CSS selectors as they are important to using jQuery. You do not need to know how to use jQuery as this book will briefly cover the basics, but it would be helpful. As long as you can understand and write simple JavaScript code, that should be sufficient to get you going. We will start off with the basics and work our way up using lots of examples.

Conventions

In this book, you will find several headings appearing frequently.

To give clear instructions of how to complete a procedure or task, we use:

Time for action – heading

1. Action 1
2. Action 2
3. Action 3

Instructions often need some extra explanation so that they make sense, so they are followed with:

What just happened?

This heading explains the working of tasks or instructions that you have just completed.

You will also find some other learning aids in the book, including:

Pop quiz – heading

These are short multiple-choice questions intended to help you test your own understanding.

Have a go hero – heading

These practical challenges give you ideas for experimenting with what you have learned.

You will also find a number of styles of text that distinguish between different kinds of information. Here are some examples of these styles, and an explanation of their meaning.

Code words in text, database table names, folder names, filenames, file extensions, pathnames, dummy URLs, user input, and Twitter handles are shown as follows: "Next, we'll add a `drawText()` method to the `Canvas2D` object."

A block of code is set as follows:

```
this.drawText = function(text, point, fill)
{
    if (fill)
    {
        context.fillText(text, point.x, point.y);
    }
```

```
        else
        {
            context.strokeText(text, point.x, point.y);
        }
};
```

When we wish to draw your attention to a particular part of a code block, the relevant lines or items are set in bold:

```
switch (action.tool)
{
    // code not shown...
    case "text":
        canvas2d.drawText(action.text, action.points[0],
            action.fill);
        break;
}
```

New terms and **important words** are shown in bold. Words that you see on the screen, in menus or dialog boxes for example, appear in the text like this: "When the **Save** button is clicked, it will get the data URL and then open it."

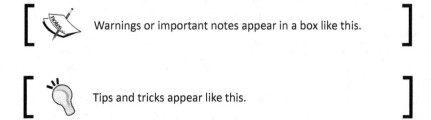

Warnings or important notes appear in a box like this.

Tips and tricks appear like this.

Reader feedback

Feedback from our readers is always welcome. Let us know what you think about this book—what you liked or may have disliked. Reader feedback is important for us to develop titles that you really get the most out of.

To send us general feedback, simply send an e-mail to feedback@packtpub.com, and mention the book title through the subject of your message.

If there is a topic that you have expertise in and you are interested in either writing or contributing to a book, see our author guide on www.packtpub.com/authors.

Customer support

Now that you are the proud owner of a Packt book, we have a number of things to help you to get the most from your purchase.

Downloading the example code

You can download the example code files for all Packt books you have purchased from your account at http://www.packtpub.com. If you purchased this book elsewhere, you can visit http://www.packtpub.com/support and register to have the files e-mailed directly to you.

Errata

Although we have taken every care to ensure the accuracy of our content, mistakes do happen. If you find a mistake in one of our books—maybe a mistake in the text or the code—we would be grateful if you would report this to us. By doing so, you can save other readers from frustration and help us improve subsequent versions of this book. If you find any errata, please report them by visiting http://www.packtpub.com/submit-errata, selecting your book, clicking on the **errata submission form** link, and entering the details of your errata. Once your errata are verified, your submission will be accepted and the errata will be uploaded to our website, or added to any list of existing errata, under the Errata section of that title.

Piracy

Piracy of copyright material on the Internet is an ongoing problem across all media. At Packt, we take the protection of our copyright and licenses very seriously. If you come across any illegal copies of our works, in any form, on the Internet, please provide us with the location address or website name immediately so that we can pursue a remedy.

Please contact us at copyright@packtpub.com with a link to the suspected pirated material.

We appreciate your help in protecting our authors, and our ability to bring you valuable content.

Questions

You can contact us at questions@packtpub.com if you are having a problem with any aspect of the book, and we will do our best to address it.

1
The Task at Hand

"I long to accomplish a great and noble task, but it is my chief duty to accomplish small tasks as if they were great and noble."

– Helen Keller

In this first chapter we will learn the basics of creating an HTML5 application. We will create an application template to be used as a starting point for building new applications quickly and with minimal effort. Then, we'll use that template to create a simple tasklist application. Along the way we will discover how to interact with the user and manipulate the application's user interface. We will also learn about our first new HTML5 feature, the Web Storage API.

In this chapter we will learn:

- The three basic components of an HTML5 application, HTML, CSS, and JavaScript
- Some jQuery basics for those of you unfamiliar with the JavaScript library
- How to initialize an application and handle user interactions
- How to manipulate the DOM to add, remove, change, and move elements
- How to create reusable HTML templates
- How to use the HTML5 Web Storage API to store and retrieve an application's state

The components of an HTML5 application

Before we get started building our first application, we need to learn some HTML5 application basics. HTML5 applications are like applications written in any other programming language. There is a certain amount of infrastructure and plumbing that needs to be put in place before we can start working on the fun part.

Web applications are pretty good when it comes to scaffolding out a project. You could just start from scratch every time you begin a new application. But as you write more and more applications, you begin to notice that you are doing the same basic things over and over every time you get started, so it makes sense to create an application template to get started up quickly without reinventing the wheel every time.

To understand how HTML5 applications are built, we will start from scratch and build our own application template which we can use when creating new applications. We will use this template as a base for all of the applications that we build throughout this book.

Every web application starts with three components: HTML, CSS, and JavaScript. You can put them all in one file, and that might be acceptable for a very simple application, but we are learning how to build real applications here. So we will start by creating three files, one for each component, and placing them in a folder named `template`. They will be named `app.html`, `app.css`, and `app.js`.

The following diagram is an interpretation of an HTML5 application and its components. Our application is built upon HTML, CSS, and JavaScript. Those in turn are built on top of CSS3 and the HTML5 framework, which consists of new markup elements and JavaScript APIs.

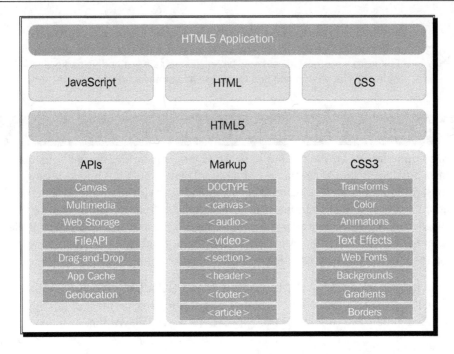

Let's look at the folder structure for our applications. We will put all of the files that we create at the root of our application's folder. We will also add a folder named `lib` which contains any third-party JavaScript libraries our application may need. Since we will always use the jQuery library, we will put a copy of it in there. If there are any other assets, such as images or audio files, we will put them in the `images` and `audio` folders respectively:

We could just reference the jQuery library from an online **content delivery network (CDN)**, but that requires you to always have an Internet connection. Take it from me, you never know when you are going to end up some place without a connection and find out you can't get any work done.

Time for action – creating the HTML file

The first component we will build is our base HTML file, app.html. We will keep our HTML as clean as possible. It should contain only markup. There should not be any styling or blocks of script mixed in it. Keeping markup, style, and behavior separated will make your applications easier to debug and maintain. For example, if there is a problem with the way something looks, we will know the problem is in the CSS file and not the JavaScript file. Another benefit is that you can completely restyle the user interface of your application by changing the CSS without ever touching its functionality.

Here is the markup for our base HTML file. All it does is include our CSS and JavaScript as well as the jQuery library, and defines a simple body structure that most of our applications will use. It is a good place to start for the applications we will be writing.

```
<!DOCTYPE html>
<html>
  <head>
    <title>App</title>
    <link href="app.css" rel="StyleSheet" />
    <script src="lib/jquery-1.8.1.min.js"></script>
    <script src="app.js"></script>
  </head>
  <body>
    <div id="app">
      <header>App</header>
      <div id="main"></div>
      <footer></footer>
    </div>
  </body>
</html>
```

 Downloading the example code

You can download the example code files for all Packt books you have purchased from your account at http://www.packtpub.com. If you purchased this book elsewhere, you can visit http://www.packtpub.com/support and register to have the files e-mailed directly to you.

One of the major differences between HTML5 markup and previous versions of HTML is the document type declaration this has been greatly simplified. As you may recall, doctypes before HTML5 were very verbose and impossible for mere mortals to remember. They looked something like this:

```
<!DOCTYPE HTML PUBLIC "-//W3C//DTD HTML 4.01//EN"
    "http://www.w3.org/TR/html4/strict.dtd">
```

Now meet the new and improved HTML5 document type declaration. It's simple, it's elegant, and best of all it's easy to remember:

```
<!DOCTYPE html>
```

Another difference you may notice are the `<header>` and `<footer>` elements. These are new semantic elements in HTML5 that are essentially the same as `<div>` elements. HTML5 actually has a whole array of new semantic elements that are designed to give HTML markup more meaning than just wrapping everything in a `<div>` tag.

Since we are building applications here and not writing content pages, we won't be focusing on these semantic elements too much. Most of the time we will use the plain old `<div>` elements. But just to familiarize you with them, here is an overview of some of the most useful new semantic elements:

- `<article>`: Defines an article in the document
- `<aside>`: Defines content aside from the other page content
- `<footer>`: Defines the footer for a section in the document
- `<header>`: Defines the header for a section in the document
- `<nav>`: Contains page navigation links
- `<section>`: Defines a section in a document

A few elements and attributes that existed in previous versions of HTML are now not present in HTML5. These are mostly elements having to do with layout and fonts, including `<big>`, `<center>`, `<font>`, `<strike>`, and `<u>`. Obsolete elements such as `<frame>` and `<applet>` are also out.

Now let's take a look at the contents of the `<body>` element in our markup. First there is a `<div id="app">` element. This will wrap the application's entire markup. Other markup, such as site navigation or anything else not related to the application, can go outside this element.

Inside the `app` element we have three more elements. Here we use a couple of the new semantic elements. First we have a `<header>` element in our application that will contain the name of the application, such as a title bar (not to be confused with the `<title>` element in the document `<head>` section). The `<div id="main">` element is where the markup for the main part of the application will go. We add a `<footer>` element below it that will be used like a status bar to display the status of the application.

Time for action – creating the CSS file

Next we'll create our base CSS file named `app.css`. This will have all of the basic styling that will be used by our applications, such as the default font and colors. The first part of the CSS file contains some document-wide element styles that set the basic look and feel.

```css
body
{
    font: 1em Verdana, Geneva, sans-serif;
    padding: 0;
    margin: 5px;
    color: Black;
    background-color: WhiteSmoke;
}
div
{
    padding: 0;
    margin: 0;
}
button
{
    cursor: pointer;
}
.hidden
{
    display: none;
}
```

First we set the style to be applied to the body, which will trickle down to the other elements. I like to set the font size to `1em` instead of a fixed pixel size so that it uses the browser's default font size. Then you can base other measurements off of that using ems or percent to give you a more reactive layout and make it easier to change the look of your application later on. Constant pixel sizes are good when you always need something to be the same size no matter what, or for small values for borders and margins, and so on.

Typically, 1em is the same as 16px by default in most browsers.

Next we make sure all padding and margins are removed from all the `div` elements, so we zero them out. It's also nice to have the cursor change to a pointer when the user hovers over a button, so we'll set that here too. Finally, there is a `.hidden` class selector that can be added to any element to hide it from being displayed.

We'll finish the CSS off with some styles for the `app` and `main` elements. All we're setting at this point are margins, padding, and colors:

```css
#app
{
    margin: 4px;
    background-color: #bbc;
}
#app>header
{
    padding: 0 0.5em;
    font-size: 1.5em;
    color: WhiteSmoke;
    background-color: #006;
}
#app>footer
{
    padding: 0.25em;
    color: WhiteSmoke;
    background-color: #006;
}
#main
{
    margin: 1em;
}
```

Time for action – creating the JavaScript file

Let's move on to the JavaScript file, `app.js`. Here we'll stub out a basic outline for our application template. If you don't know what the dollar signs are for, they are aliases for the jQuery library. We'll go over some jQuery basics in a moment.

```javascript
"use strict";

function MyApp()
```

```
{
    var version = "v1.0";

    function setStatus(message)
    {
        $("#app>footer").text(message);
    }

    this.start = function()
    {
        $("#app>header").append(version);
        setStatus("ready");
    };
}
```

Starting at the top we will include `"use strict"` in our JavaScript files. This informs the JavaScript runtime to use newer and stricter standards when running our code. For example, in older versions of JavaScript it was completely legal to use a variable name without declaring it first using the `var` keyword. This had the side effect of making it a global variable attached to the `window` object. When `"use strict"` is defined, you will get an error if you try to do that. It helps you find bad coding mistakes that could lead to bugs in your program.

If you are using some older JavaScript library that doesn't work in strict mode you can add `"use strict"` inside of function declarations instead, to make only that block of code use strict mode.

```
function strict()
{
    "use strict";
    // Everything inside here will use strict
// mode
}
```

Next we define the main application object, `myApp`. There are many ways to define an object in JavaScript, including using object literals and constructor functions. Object literals are the simplest way to define an object, but those objects are created as soon as the JavaScript is loaded, usually before the DOM is ready. Here's what our object would look like as an object literal:

```
var myApp = {
    version: "v1.0",
    setStatus: function(message)
    {
        $("#app>footer").text(message);
    },
```

```
    start: function()
    {
        $("#app>header").append(this.version);
        this.setStatus("ready");
    };
};
```

Since our applications are manipulating the Document Object Model (DOM), we don't want to create the object until the DOM is ready. That's why we will be using the function constructor form for creating an object.

The **DOM**, or **Document Object Model**, is the internal representation of the HTML markup. It's a hierarchical tree of objects that represents the HTML elements.

Another problem with using object literals is that everything defined in it is a member of the object, and therefore must be accessed using the `this` keyword. Notice in the preceding object literal form how we must use `this` to access `version` and `setStatus()`. However, when creating an object using a constructor, we can define functions and variables inside of the constructor without making them members of the object. Since they aren't members, you don't have to use the `this` keyword to access them.

So what's wrong with using `this`? After you've programmed in JavaScript for a while, you become aware that the `this` keyword can cause a lot of confusion because it can mean different things at different times. In other languages, such as C# and Java, `this` always points to the object that you are inside of. In JavaScript, `this` is a pointer to the object that called the function, which for event handlers is usually the `window` object. So the more we avoid using it, the better.

Another advantage of using a constructor is being able to define private and public methods. Notice that the `setStatus()` method is defined using a normal function declaration. This will make it a private method that can only be accessed from within the object that encloses it, and doesn't require using `this` to call it. The `start()` method, on the other hand, is assigned to the object using `this`. That will make `start()` a public method that can only be accessed from an instance of the object. We will use this paradigm throughout our JavaScript to implement the private and public members of our objects.

The last thing we need is a document-ready event handler. The document-ready event gets fired once the page has loaded and the DOM hierarchy has been fully constructed. There are two ways to add this event handler using jQuery. The first and more verbose way is what you would expect:

```
$(document).ready(handler);
```

However, since it is probably the most basic and important event you will need to implement, jQuery provides a shorthand form that is as simple as it gets:

```
$(handler);
```

Here is our document-ready event handler:

```
$(function() {
    window.app = new MyApp();
    window.app.start();
});
```

This is an important piece of code. It defines the starting point for our application. It is equivalent to the main() function in other languages, such as C, C++, C#, and Java.

Here we create an instance of our main application object, and then assign it to a global variable named app by attaching it to the window object. We make it global so it can be accessed throughout our application. Last but not least we call the start() method of our application object to get the application going.

What just happened?

We just created a template that we can use to start writing new applications with minimal startup time. It consists of HTML, CSS, and JavaScript files. At this point our template is finished, and we have the basics we will need to start writing new HTML5 applications.

The dollar sign identifier

You may have noticed dollar signs everywhere in our JavaScript code. The dollar sign is no more than an alias for the jQuery object. You could replace all dollar signs with jQuery and it would be the same, just more typing. If you already know about jQuery you might want to jump ahead. Otherwise I'll give a brief overview of jQuery.

jQuery is a popular JavaScript library that at its most basic level provides functions to access and manipulate the DOM. It also provides a lot of other useful functionality, such as event handling, animations, and AJAX support. In addition, it hides many of the different quirks between browsers, so you can concentrate on programming and not on how to make your code work in every browser. It makes writing JavaScript applications tolerable, and dare I say fun. I wouldn't think of writing an HTML5 application without it. It's to JavaScript what the System library is to Java and C#.

For the most part, jQuery uses the same query syntax as CSS to select elements. The typical pattern is to select one or more elements and then perform some action on them, or retrieve data from them. So, for example, here is a jQuery select to get all `div` elements in the DOM:

```
$("div")
```

The following query would give you the element that has an ID of `main`:

```
$("#main")
```

Just like CSS, the hash sign selects elements with a specific ID, and a dot selects elements that have a specific class. You can also use compound search criteria. This next query would return all of the elements that are descendants of the element with an ID of `main` and have a class of `selected`:

```
$(#main .selected")
```

After you have selected one or more elements you can perform some action on them. A jQuery select returns a jQuery object that is like an array, but also has lots of built-in functions to do all sorts of things, which we will learn about as we progress through this book. For example, the following line of code would hide all of the elements returned from the previous select (set their CSS `display` attribute to `none`):

```
$(#main .selected").hide()
```

Simple and powerful. So what is the deal with the dollar sign anyway? Some people assumed it was some sort of magic that jQuery could use the dollar sign as an alias. But apparently the dollar sign is a valid character to start a variable or function name within JavaScript.

Creating our first application

Throughout this and the next couple of chapters, we will be building a tasklist application that uses HTML5 and CSS3. Before we get started we should spell out the specifications for our application so we know what we want to build.

◆ Our tasklist application should allow the user to quickly type in one or more task names and display them in a list.

◆ The user should be able to easily manipulate the tasks by editing them, deleting them, or moving them up or down in the order of the list.

◆ The application should remember the tasks that were entered, so when the user comes back to it they can continue where they left off.

◆ The UI should be reactive so that it can be used on a number of different devices with different screen sizes.

◆ We will start off simple and build upon what we've done as we go along. Throughout the process we will build some JavaScript libraries that can be used in subsequent projects, so we can hit the ground running.

Time for action – creating a tasklist

Now that we have the basics under our belt let's get started on the tasklist application. We'll call our application Task at Hand, or Task@Hand to be hip. First make a copy of our template folder and rename it to taskAtHand. Also rename the .html, .css, and .js files to taskAtHand. Now we're ready to start our first HTML5 application. You can find the code for this section in Chapter 1/example1.1.

The first thing we need to do is go into the HTML file and change the title and names of the CSS and JS files in the <head> element to taskAtHand:

```
<head>
  <title>Task@Hand</title>
  <link href="taskAtHand.css" rel="StyleSheet" />
  <script src="lib/jquery-1.8.1.min.js"></script>
  <script src="taskAtHand.js"></script>
</head>
```

Next we move on to the body. First we change the name of the application in the <header> element. Then go into the <div id="app"> element and add a text input field where the user can type in the name of a task. Finally, we add an empty list to hold our list of tasks. Since we are building a list we will use the unordered list <ul> element.

```
<body>
  <div id="app">
    <header>Task@Hand</header>
    <div id="main">
      <div id="add-task">
        <label for="new-task-name">Add a task</label>
        <input type="text" id="new-task-name"
          title="Enter a task name" placeholder="Enter a task name"/>
      </div>
      <ul id="task-list">
      </ul>
    </div>
    <footer>
    </footer>
  </div>
</body>
```

That's all of the markup we need for now. There is one thing to point out in here, that's new to HTML5. There is a new attribute for inputs called `placeholder` that displays some text in the field until the user starts typing something. This gives the user a hint as to what they should enter in the field. It is valid for input elements that allow the user to enter text.

Let's go into the JavaScript file and get coding. The first thing we'll do is rename the application object to `TaskAtHandApp`:

```
function TaskAtHandApp()
{
    // code not shown...
}
$(function() {
    window.app = new TaskAtHandApp();
    window.app.start();
});
```

 A standard in JavaScript is that only things that require a new statement (that is, object constructors) should start with a capital letter. This helps to distinguish what requires the new keyword to be created. Everything else, including variable and function names, should start with a lowercase letter.

When the user is done typing in a task name and hits the *Enter* key, we want to create a new list item element and add it to the list. The first thing we need to do is add an event handler to the text field so we get notified when a key is pressed. We will add this in the `start()` method of our application object:

```
this.start = function()
{
    $("#new-task-name").keypress(function(e) {
        if (e.which == 13) // Enter key
        {
            addTask();
            return false;
        }
    })
    .focus();

    $("#app header").append(version);
    setStatus("ready");
};
```

First we get the text field by doing a jQuery select on its ID, `new-task-name`. Then we add a `keypress()` event handler to that element passing in a function to execute every time the event is triggered. jQuery passes one parameter to the event handler function, which is a `keypress` event object. The event object contains a field named `which` that contains the character code of the key that was pressed. The one we are interested in here is the *Enter* key, which has a code of `13`.

When the user presses the *Enter* key we call the `addTask()` method (defined next), and then it returns `false`. The reason we return `false` here is to tell the system that we handled the key press event, and don't want it to do the default action. Some browsers will perform other actions when the *Enter* key is pressed.

Next, we add another function call onto the end of the `keypress()` handler to set the focus back to the text field. At this point you're probably asking yourself, how does that work, calling a function on a function? This is called function chaining and is perhaps one of the most useful features of jQuery. Most of jQuery's methods return a pointer to the object itself, so we can perform multiple actions in a single line of code.

Now we'll write that `addTask()` method. This method will get the name of the task and add a new list item to the `<ul>` element in our HTML:

```
function addTask()
{
    var taskName = $("#new-task-name").val();
    if (taskName)
    {
        addTaskElement(taskName);
        // Reset the text field
        $("#new-task-name").val("").focus();
    }
}
function addTaskElement(taskName)
{
    var $task = $("<li></li>");
    $task.text(taskName);
    $("#task-list").append($task);
}
```

First we get the value of the `new-task-name` text field using jQuery's `val()` method, which is used to get the value of input fields. Just to make sure the user actually typed something in, we test that the `taskName` variable is "truthy", which in this case means it's not an empty string.

Next we call the `addTaskElement()` method. There we create a new `<li>` element. You can create a new element by passing in an element definition instead of select to jQuery. In this case we use `"<li></li>"` to create a new empty list item element, and then assign it to the `$task` variable. Then, we immediately fill that element with the task name using the `text()` method.

 When assigning a jQuery object to a variable, it's a good practice to start the variable name with `$`, so you know that it references a jQuery object.

Now that we have the new element we need to add it to the document in the correct place, which is inside the `<ul id="task-list">` element. That is done by selecting the `task-list` element and calling the `append()` method. This adds our new `<li>` element to the end of the tasklist.

The last thing we do, back in the `addTask()` method, is clear out the value of the text input field and set the focus back on it so the user can immediately enter another task. We use function chaining here to do both in one statement. Notice that we used the jQuery `val()` method for both setting and getting the value of the text field. If you pass a value in, it sets the control's value; otherwise it returns the control's value. You'll find that a lot of the jQuery methods work this way. For example, the `text()` method will either set the text within an element, or return it if no value is passed in.

What just happened?

We created a tasklist application where the user can type in task names and build a list of tasks. Let's open the application in our browser and see what we've got so far:

Time for action – removing a task from the list

Now that we can add tasks to the list, let's add the ability to remove tasks. To do this we'll need a delete button for each task in the list. We'll add the code to create the button in the `addTaskElement()` method. You can find the code for this section in Chapter 1/example1.2.

```
function addTaskElement(taskName)
{
    var $task = $("<li></li>");
    var $delete = $("<button class='delete'>X</button>");
    $task.append($delete)
        .append("<span class='task-name'>" + taskName +
                "</span>");
    $delete.click(function() { $task.remove(); });
}
```

The first thing this method does is create a new `<button>` element with a class of `delete`. Then it creates the list item element as we did before, except that first it appends the delete button and then appends the task name. Note that we are now wrapping the task name in a `<span class='task-name'>` element to help us keep track of it. Last we add a click event handler to the delete button. To delete the task from the list element we simply call the `remove()` method to remove it from the DOM. Voila, it's gone!

Time for action – moving tasks within the list

While we're at it, let's add buttons to move tasks up and down in the list. For this we'll add some more code to the `addTaskElement()` method. First we need to create `move-up` and `move-down` buttons, and then add them to the list element along with the `delete` button.

```
function addTaskElement(taskName)
{
    var $task = $("<li></li>");
    var $delete = $("<button class='delete'>X</button>");
    var $moveUp = $("<button class='move-up'>^</button>");
    var $moveDown = $("<button class='move-up'>v</button>");
    $task.append($delete)
        .append($moveUp)
        .append($moveDown)
        .append("<span class='task-name'>" + taskName +
                "</span>");
    $("#task-list").append($task);

    $delete.click(function() { $task.remove(); });
```

```
        $moveUp.click(function() {
            $task.insertBefore($task.prev());
        });
        $moveDown.click(function() {
            $task.insertAfter($task.next());
        });
    }
```

When the **move up** or **move down** button is clicked, it finds the previous or next task element using the `prev()` and `next()` methods. Then it uses the jQuery `insertBefore()` and `insertAfter()` methods to move the task element up or down in the tasklist.

What just happened?

We added buttons to each task element so that we can delete them or move them up and down in the order of the list. We learned how to use the jQuery `remove()`, `insertBefore()`, and `insertAfter()` methods to modify the DOM.

HTML templates

As you can see, things are getting a little messy in our `addTaskElement()` method. We are creating a bunch of elements programmatically in JavaScript and manually adding them to the DOM. Wouldn't it be a lot easier if we could just define what we want the task element's structure to look like in our HTML file and use it to create new tasks? Well we can, and we will. In this section we'll create an HTML template that we can reuse to easily create new tasks.

 There are plenty of JavaScript libraries out there for implementing HTML templates and they have a lot of powerful features, but for our application all we need is something simple, so we'll implement our own.

Time for action – implementing a template

To start out we need a place to put the template's markup. So we'll add a `<div id="templates">` to our HTML file outside of the app element and give it a class of `hidden`. As you may recall from our CSS, the hidden class sets `display` to `none` for an element. This will hide the template's markup so it is never seen by the user. Now let's define the template:

```
<div id="app">
   ...
</div>
<div id="templates" class="hidden">
  <ul id="task-template">
    <li class="task">
```

```
        <div class="tools">
          <button class="delete" title="Delete">X</button>
          <button class="move-up" title="Up">^</button>
          <button class="move-down" title="Down">v</button>
        </div>
        <span class="task-name"></span>
      </li>
    </ul>
  </div>
```

I don't know about you, but for me that's a lot easier than trying to build the task elements in the code. It's also a lot easier to read, add to, and maintain. You may have noticed a few other elements and attributes were added that would have been painful to add programmatically. A `<div class="tools">` was placed around the buttons to group them together, and a `title` attribute was added to each button that will show up as tool tips in the browser.

Note that we did not use any ID attributes anywhere in the task elements. Instead we are using class attributes to identify different elements. The reason for this is that an ID uniquely identifies an element, so it should only be used once. If we create a template that has a bunch of IDs and start copying it, we will have duplicate IDs. An ID is pretty worthless for uniquely identifying an element if you use it more than once.

Before we move on, we need to add some styling to our CSS for the buttons and their container. We want the buttons to remain on the same line as the task name but their container `<div>` is a block-level element. Let's change it to `inline-block` so it doesn't break:

```
#task-list .task .tools
{
    display: inline-block;
}
```

We also want to remove the borders from the buttons, make them all the same size, and remove padding and margins so it's more compact:

```
#task-list .task .tools button
{
    margin: 0;
    padding: 0;
    width: 1.25em;
    height: 1.25em;
    border: none;
}
```

So, now that we have a task template what do we do with it? jQuery comes in handy here again. All we have to do is get the template element and use the `clone()` method to make a copy of it. Then insert the copy wherever we want to in the DOM. Here's what our new `addTaskElement()` method looks like:

```
function addTaskElement(taskName)
{
    var $task = $("#task-template .task").clone();
    $("span.task-name", $task).text(taskName);

    $("#task-list").append($task);

    $("button.delete", $task).click(function() {
        $task.remove();
    });
    $("button.move-up", $task).click(function() {
        $task.insertBefore($task.prev());
    });
    $("button.move-down", $task).click(function() {
        $task.insertAfter($task.next());
    });
}
```

We've replaced all those lines of creating elements with one line of code that gets the task template element and makes a copy of it using the `clone()` method. The second line fills the task name into the `<span class="task-name">` element we have set up to hold it. If you look closely you will see that we are passing in a second parameter to jQuery in our select now. That tells jQuery to only search for elements that are descendants of the `task` element. Otherwise it would find every task name element in the document and change it. We do the same thing when selecting the buttons to hook up click event handlers to them, using their class name to identify them.

What just happened?

We implemented an HTML template that allows us to remove all of the code to dynamically generate task elements and replace it with a call to jQuery's `clone()` method. This makes it easier for us to update and maintain element structures in HTML rather than JavaScript.

Time for action – editing a task in the list

So far we have a tasklist that we can add tasks to, remove tasks from, and change the order of the tasks. Let's add some functionality to allow the user to change the name of a task. When the user clicks on a task name we will change it to a text input field. To do that we need to add a text input field to our task element template right after the task name:

```
<li class="task">
    <div class="tools">
        <button class="delete" title="Delete">X</button>
        <button class="move-up" title="Up">^</button>
        <button class="move-down" title="Down">v</button>
    </div>
    <span class="task-name"></span>
    <input type="text" class="task-name hidden"/>
</li>
```

We give it a class of task-name to identify it, and also add the hidden class so it's not visible by default. We only want to show it when the user clicks on the task name. So let's go into the JavaScript file and add an event handler on the <span> element to the end of our addTaskElement() method:

```
$("span.task-name", $task).click(function() {
    onEditTaskName($(this));
});
```

Let's break this down. First we get the span with the class of task-name that is a child of the task element. Then we add a click event handler that calls the onEditTaskName() method. The onEditTaskName() method takes a reference to the <span> element as a parameter. When you are in a jQuery event handler function, this refers to the element that was the source of the event. So $(this) creates a jQuery object that wraps the <span> element so we can call jQuery methods on it:

```
function onEditTaskName($span)
{
    $span.hide()
        .siblings("input.task-name")
        .val($span.text())
        .show()
        .focus();
}
```

Even though the `onEditTaskName()` method technically contains one line of code, there is a lot going on. It uses function chaining to do a lot of work in a compact statement. First it hides the `<span>` element. Then it gets the text input field by looking for a sibling of the `<span>` element, that is, an `<input>` element with a class of `task-name`. Then it sets the value of the text field with the task name which it gets from the `<span>` element using jQuery's `text()` method. Finally, it makes the text field visible and sets the focus on it.

When the user clicks on the task name, it appears to change into an editable text field right before their eyes. Now all we need is a way to change it back when the user is done editing the name. To do that we'll add a change event handler to the text field, which gets fired when the user changes the text field and hits *Enter* or leaves it. Add this to the end of the `addTaskElement()` method:

```
$("input.task-name", $task).change(function() {
    onChangeTaskName($(this));
});
```

This works the same way as the task name click event handler. We are going to call a method named `onChangeTaskName()` and pass it a jQuery object that wraps the text field's input element:

```
function onChangeTaskName($input)
{
    $input.hide();
    var $span = $input.siblings("span.task-name");
    if ($input.val())
    {
        $span.text($input.val());
    }
    $span.show();
}
```

First we hide the text input field, and then get the task name `<span>` element and store it in a variable. Before updating the name we check to make sure that the user actually typed something in. If so, we update the task name. Finally, we call `show()` to make the task name visible again. The user sees the text field turn back into static text.

There is one last thing left to do. If the user clicks off the field without changing anything, we will not get a change event and the text field will not get hidden. We can get a blur event when this happens though. So let's add a blur event handler to the text field that hides it and shows the static task name <span> element:

```
$("input.task-name", $task).change(function() {
    onChangeTaskName($(this));
})
.blur(function() {
    $(this).hide().siblings("span.task-name").show();
});
```

What just happened?

We added a text field to our task template that gets shown when the user clicks on the task name, so they can edit the task name. When the task name text field changes, it updates the task name label.

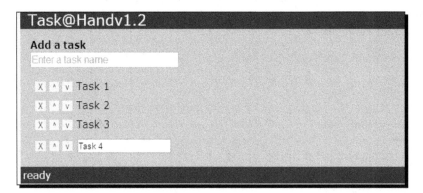

Saving the state of the application

We have a pretty functional tasklist application now. We can add, remove, and move tasks around. We can even edit the name of an existing task. There's only one problem. Since we added all of these task elements to the DOM dynamically, they won't be there the next time the user comes back to the application. We need a way to save the tasklist, so the next time the user comes back to the application the tasks will still be there. Otherwise, what's the point?

HTML5 has just the thing for that-Web Storage. Web Storage is a new API in HTML5 that allows you to store information on the client. In the past, the only kind of storage available on the client was cookies. But cookies aren't a great way to store data on the client. They are limited to only a few kilobytes of data and are also included in HTTP requests, inflating their size.

Web Storage, on the other hand, allows us to save much more data (up to 5 MB in most browsers) and adds nothing to the HTTP requests. It consists of two global objects that have the same interface, localStorage and sessionStorage. The only difference between the two is that data stored in sessionStorage goes away when the browser is closed, while data stored in localStorage doesn't. Since we want to save application data between sessions we will only use localStorage.

Data is stored as key/value pairs. You can set values using the setItem() method and retrieve values using getItem() as follows:

```
localStorage.setItem("myKey", "myValue");
var value = localStorage.getItem("myKey") // returns "myValue"
```

If you try to get a value using a key that doesn't exist in localStorage, it will return null. If you try to add a value to localStorage and there is not enough memory left, you will get a QUOTA_EXCEEDED_ERR exception.

There are a few limitations to localStorage:

- The user doesn't necessarily have access to anything stored there (although it can be accessed through the browser's developer tools).

- It is shared by all applications in a domain, so the storage limit is shared among all of your applications. This also means that all of your keys among all of your applications must be unique. If two applications use the same key they will end up overwriting each other's data.

- Both keys and values must be strings. If you want to store something that is not a string, you must convert it to a string first. When you pull that value out of storage you must convert it back from a string to the type you're expecting.

Fortunately for us, JavaScript has a utility object called JSON that provides functions to convert values to and from strings. **JSON** stands for **JavaScript Object Notation** and is the standard for representing values as strings in a readable format. It is a subset of object literal notation in JavaScript, so if you know how to define object literals you know JSON. The JSON object has two methods; JSON.stringify() to convert a value to a string, and JSON.parse() to convert a string back into a value.

Time for action – creating a localStorage wrapper

To help get around some of the limitations of `localStorage` we are going to create an object called `AppStorage` that provides a wrapper over the `localStorage` object. The `AppStorage` object will help us avoid key collisions and provide an easy way to store non-string values. Let's define this object in a new file called `appStorage.js`, so we can reuse it in all of our applications. You can find the code for this section in `Chapter 1/example1.3`.

```
function AppStorage(appName)
{
    var prefix = (appName ? appName + "." : "");
```

The constructor takes in the application name as a parameter. The next line sets a private variable named `prefix` that will be used to prefix all of our keys with the application name to avoid collisions. If an `appName` parameter is not provided, it will not use a prefix, which could be useful for data shared among all your applications. If we pass in `"myApp"` to the constructor, all of the keys for our app will start with `"myApp"` (for example, `myApp.settings` or `myApp.data`).

This next line creates a public variable that is used to determine if `localStorage` is supported by the browser. It simply checks to see if the global `localStorage` object exists:

```
this.localStorageSupported = (('localStorage' in window) &&
window['localStorage']);
```

Let's implement the `setValue()` method used to set values in local storage first:

```
this.setValue = function(key, val)
{
    if (this.localStorageSupported)
        localStorage.setItem(prefix + key, JSON.stringify(val));
    return this;
};
```

The `setValue()` method takes a key and a value to put into local storage. It prepends the application prefix to the key to help avoid naming collisions. Since you can only put strings into local storage we use the `JSON.stringify()` method to convert the value to a string, and then call `localStorage.setItem()` to store it.

Now let's implement the `getValue()` method to get values from `localStorage`:

```
this.getValue = function(key)
{
    if (this.localStorageSupported)
        return JSON.parse(localStorage.getItem(prefix + key));
    else return null;
};
```

The getValue() method takes a key, prepends the prefix to it, and returns the string value associated with it in localStorage. It uses JSON.parse() to parse the string retrieved from localStorage into a value. If the key doesn't exist or local storage is not supported, these methods return null.

The next thing we need is a way to remove items. Let's implement the removeValue() method to do that. It simply calls localStorage.removeItem() passing in the prefixed key:

```
this.removeValue = function(key)
{
    if (this.localStorageSupported)
        localStorage.removeItem(prefix + key);
    return this;
};
```

While we're at it, let's add a method to remove all keys for an application. localStorage does have a clear() method, but that completely empties out localStorage for your domain, not just the values for our application. So we need to get all of the keys for our application and then delete them one-by-one:

```
this.removeAll = function()
{
    var keys = this.getKeys();
    for (var i in keys)
    {
        this.remove(keys[i]);
    }
    return this;
};
```

The removeAll() method references a getKeys() method. This method will return an array of all key names for the application. We will make the getKeys() method, so the user can also pass in a filter function to further filter the results by their own criteria if they wish:

```
this.getKeys = function(filter)
{
    var keys = [];
    if (this.localStorageSupported)
    {
        for (var key in localStorage)
        {
            if (isAppKey(key))
            {
                // Remove the prefix from the key
                if (prefix) key = key.slice(prefix.length);
                // Check the filter
```

```
                    if (!filter || filter(key))
                    {
                        keys.push(key);
                    }
                }
            }
        }
        return keys;
    };
    function isAppKey(key)
    {
        if (prefix)
        {
            return key.indexOf(prefix) === 0;
        }
        return true;
    };
```

This method works by looping over all of the keys in `localStorage`, which you can get in the same way that you get all of the keys in an object or array, by implementing a loop using the `in` keyword. It calls the private method `isAppKey()` to determine if the key belongs to our application. If so, it removes the application prefix from the key. Lastly, if no filter is defined or the filter function returns `true`, add the key to the array of keys to pass back.

The private `isAppKey()` method takes a key name as the parameter and returns `true` if the key belongs to our application. If an application name prefix is not defined there's nothing to check. Otherwise we check to see if the key starts with the application prefix.

There's one last public method we need to write. The `contains()` method will determine if there is a value associated with a key. It simply tries to get the value associated with the key and checks to see if it exists:

```
    this.contains = function(key)
    {
        return this.get(key) !== null;
    };
```

What just happened?

We created a wrapper object called `AppStorage` over the HTML5 `localStorage` object. It encapsulates all of the behavior for interacting with `localStorage` and saving JavaScript objects to it. Now we can save any type of data to `localStorage` and then retrieve it.

Time for action – storing the tasklist

Let's get back to the tasklist application. First we'll add a reference to `appStorage.js` in our HTML file:

```
<script src="appStorage.js"></script>
```

Next we'll add a private `appStorage` variable to the `TaskAtHandApp` object, passing in the name of the application to the constructor:

```
function TaskAtHandApp()
{
    var version = "v1.3",
        appStorage = new AppStorage("taskAtHand");
    //…
}
```

Now let's add a private method that can be called to save the tasks whenever a change is made:

```
function saveTaskList()
{
    var tasks = [];
    $("#task-list .task span.task-name").each(function() {
        tasks.push($(this).text())
    });
    appStorage.setValue("taskList", tasks);
}
```

The `saveTaskList()` method finds all of the task name `<span>` elements for each task in the list. Then it calls the jQuery `each()` method, which is used to iterate over the elements that were found by the select. The `each()` method takes a function as a parameter and calls that function for each element. Our function simply pushes the task name onto the end of the tasks array. Then we call `appStorage.setValue()` telling it to store the tasks array using the key `"taskList"`.

Now we need to add a call to `saveTaskList()` every time the list changes. That would be in the `addTask()` and `onChangeTaskName()` methods. Also, in `addTaskElement()` we need to call it from the button click event handlers for `delete`, `move-up`, and `move-down`. To make things easier to read, let's do a little refactoring for the button event handlers by moving the inline handler code out to private methods:

```
function addTaskElement(taskName)
{
    // code not shown…
    $("button.delete", $task).click(function() {
```

```
            removeTask($task);
        });
        $("button.move-up", $task).click(function() {
            moveTask($task, true);
        });
        $("button.move-down", $task).click(function() {
            moveTask($task, false);
        });
        //...
    }
    function removeTask($task)
    {
        $task.remove();
        saveTaskList();
    }
    function moveTask($task, moveUp)
    {
        if (moveUp)
        {
            $task.insertBefore($task.prev());
        }
        else
        {
            $task.insertAfter($task.next());
        }
        saveTaskList();
    }
```

Let's take a look at this in Chrome now. Go ahead and add a few tasks then press *F12* to open developer tools. If you click on the **Resources** icon at the top of the window you will see a list of resources in the left pane. Expand the **Local Storage** item and click on the item under it. You should see all of the data that is stored in local storage for your domain in the right pane:

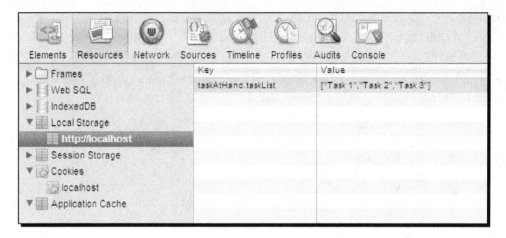

In the **Key** column you should find `taskAtHand.taskList` and see the JSON that represents our list of tasks in the **Value** column, which as you may recall is stored as an array.

Now go ahead and play around with it. Try adding, removing, editing, and moving tasks around. You should see the value in local storage get updated after every change. We now have a persistent tasklist.

Some browsers don't allow access to `localStorage` when using the `file://` protocol (that is, you opened the file directly from the file system into your browser). If your `localStorage` isn't working, try it in another web browser or access your application through a web server, such as IIS or Apache.

Time for action – loading the tasklist

We have the tasklist saved. But that doesn't do us much good if we can't load it. So let's add a new private method called `loadTaskList()`:

```
function loadTaskList()
{
    var tasks = appStorage.getObject("taskList");
    if (tasks)
    {
        for (var i in tasks)
        {
            addTaskElement(tasks[i]);
        }
    }
}
```

This method calls `appStorage.getValue()` passing in the key for our tasklist. Then it checks to make sure we got something back. If so, it iterates over all of the tasks in the array calling the `addTaskElement()` method for each one.

The only thing left to do is add a call to `loadTaskList()` from the `start()` method, so the list is loaded when the application starts:

```
this.start = function()
{
    // Code not shown...
    loadTaskList();
    setStatus("ready");
};
```

What just happened?

We used the `AppStorage` object in our tasklist application to store the tasklist to `localStorage` any time something changes, and then retrieve it and build the tasklist when the user returns.

Have a go hero

Write a local storage browser application that can be used to look at the data for each application in your domain. At the top level, list all of the applications. When you drill down into the application, it shows all of its local storage items. When you click an item, it shows the contents of that item.

Pop quiz

Q1. What are the three basic components of an HTML5 application?

1. jQuery, templates, and local storage
2. Document, object, and model
3. Tags, elements, and attributes
4. HTML, CSS, and JavaScript

Q2. What type of data can be stored in local storage?

1. Any type
2. Objects
3. Numbers
4. Strings

Summary

There you have it. We now have our first HTML5 application under our belts. A tasklist where we can add, remove, and edit tasks. The tasks are persisted, so that when the user returns to the application they can continue from where they left off. We covered the following concepts in this chapter:

◆ We learned the basics of building an HTML5 application and its three components, HTML, CSS, and JS

◆ We created an application template to help us get new applications started quickly

◆ We learned how to use jQuery to access and manipulate the DOM

◆ We learned how to initialize a web application and handle user interaction

◆ We learned how to create HTML templates so we can define reusable element structures in markup

◆ We learned how to use Web Storage to save and retrieve the state of an application, and created an `AppStorage` object to help us access `localStorage`

Now that we've learned the basics of creating HTML5 applications and have our tasklist application working, we're ready to do some styling. In the next chapter, we will learn about some of the new CSS3 features that will make our application look as good, or better than, any desktop app.

2
Let's Get Stylish

"In matters of style, swim with the current; in matters of principle, stand like a rock." – Thomas Jefferson

In this chapter, we will put on our graphic designer hats and do some styling. Right now our task list application that we created in the first chapter works but it looks like something from 2005. We will bring it up to the present and into the future using CSS3 to give it a clean, modern look. We will add rounded corners, shadows, gradients, and transitions using the latest CSS3 features.
We will also use CSS sprites to add some images to the task list buttons.

In this chapter we will learn:

- New ways to specify colors in CSS3 and set transparencies
- How to add rounded corners to elements
- How to add shadows to elements and text
- How to draw gradients in element backgrounds
- New CSS3 background properties
- How to use CSS sprites in your applications
- How to use transitions and transforms to add effects to the user interface
- How to dynamically load stylesheets to create customizable user interfaces

CSS3 overview

CSS3 is not part of the HTML5 specification, but it is an integral part of writing HTML5 applications. CSS3 is being developed in tandem with HTML5 and provides many new styles to make web pages look and function better than ever. Things that were once the realm of Photoshop, such as gradients and shadows, are now easily added via styling. Using these new graphics features will make your applications look modern and add character to your applications.

Some of the most exciting additions to CSS are the ability to add gradients and shadows to elements. Rounded corners, a feature that everyone wanted in their web pages, and which were once the realm of many HTML hacks, are now simple to add. It has never been easier to make web pages and applications look good without having to download extra images and code to support them.

You can see examples of all the following CSS3 styles in `chapter2/css3-examples/css3-examples.html`.

CSS3 colors

Before we get started with the new effects, let's discuss colors. CSS3 has new ways to define colors that allow you to set transparency and define colors in HSL format. Of course, you can still use the old standards of hex values, any of the CSS color names, and the `rgb()` specifier.

A new `rgba()` specifier has been added to allow the alpha, or opacity amount, to be set with a color. Just like `rgb()`, the first three parameters set red, green, and blue amounts, and are values ranging from 0 to 255. A fourth parameter, the alpha, is a floating point value from 0 to 1 where 0 is completely transparent and 1 is completely opaque. The following declares a red background color that is 50 percent transparent:

```
background-color: rgba(255, 0, 0, 0.5);
```

Although most browsers support `rgba()`, it's a good idea to specify a fallback for those that don't support it by defining a color in `rgb()` format preceding it, as shown here:

```
background-color: rgb(255, 0, 0);
background-color: rgba(255, 0, 0, 0.5);
```

Here's an example of overlapping three elements all with an alpha value of 0.5 and having colors red, green, and blue (yes, you can draw circular elements, which we'll see in the next section):

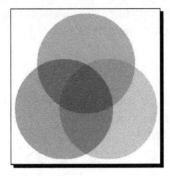

In addition to RGB colors, CSS3 also supports **HSL** colors, which stands for **Hue**, **Saturation**, and **Lightness**. HSL is based on a color wheel that is full color at the edges and fades to gray in the center. Now extend the wheel into a cylinder that is black at the bottom, white at the top, and full color in the middle. That is the theory around HSL colors.

It is specified using `hsl(h, s, l)`. Hue is a value from 0 to 360 that maps to the degrees on the color wheel. 0 is red, 120 is green, 240 is blue, and 360 is back around to red. Saturation is the percentage of color where 0% is completely gray and 100% full color. Lightness is the percent of lightness where 0% is black, 50% is full color, and 100% is white. You can specify it with or without an alpha value, the same as `rgb()`, as shown here:

```
hsl(240, 100%, 50%);
hsla(240, 100%, 50%, 0.5);
```

Most people don't think of colors in HSL, but it's out there just in case you want to use it. If you want to play around with it, there is a nice HSL picker at `http://hslpicker.com`.

Rounded corners

The first CSS3 effect that we'll look at is rounded corners, since that was such a sought-after feature before CSS3. In the past, if you wanted rounded corners, there were only a few non-optimal solutions available. You could load four images, one for each corner, and add some extra markup to get them to line up (and try to make it work in all browsers). Or implement some kind of hack using multiple `div` tags to "draw" a rounded border. Or one of a half a dozen other ways. In the end none of them were great solutions. So why did we go to such lengths to make rounded corners work before CSS3? Because people are attracted to them and they just seem to make your design look more natural.

Rounded corners are ridiculously easy to add to elements using CSS3's new `border-radius` property. If you want each corner to have the same border radius, just give it one value, like this:

```
border-radius: 0.5em;
```

If you want to set each corner of the border to a different radius, you can do that too. The values are in the standard order for CSS properties, clockwise from the top-left: top-left, top-right, bottom-right, and bottom-left.

```
border-radius: 1px 4px 8px 12px;
```

You may set one, two, three, or all four values. One and four are self-explanatory.

- If two values are set, the first applies to top-left and bottom-right and the second applies to top-right and bottom-left. So it's opposite corners.

- If three values are set, the second value applies to top-right and bottom-left. The first applies to top-left and the third to bottom-right.

You can also define each corner's radius separately, as shown here:

```
border-top-left-radius: 1px;
border-top-right-radius: 4px;
border-bottom-right-radius: 8px;
border-bottom-left-radius: 12px;
```

 Want to create a circle or ellipse? Set the `border-radius` value to 50%.

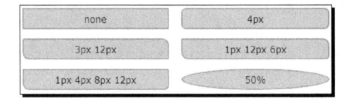

Shadows

Adding shadows to elements and text is simple in CSS3. Use shadows to make certain elements really stand out and give a more natural look to your UI. There are many options for adding shadows, such as size, position, and color. Shadows don't always have to be behind elements and text; they can frame, highlight, and add effects to them too.

Box shadows

In addition to rounded corners, you can add shadows to elements using the new CSS3 `box-shadow` property. The `box-shadow` property takes a number of parameters that tells it how to draw the shadow:

```
box-shadow: h-offset v-offset blur-radius spread-radius color;
```

Here is an explanation of the parameters:

- `h-offset`: The horizontal offset of the shadow. Negative values put the shadow to the left of the element.
- `v-offset`: The vertical offset of the shadow. Negative values put the shadow above the element.
- `blur-radius`: Determines the blur amount; the higher the number, the more blur (optional).
- `spread-radius`: The size of the shadow. If zero, it's the same size as the blur (optional).
- `color`: The color of the shadow (optional).
- `inset`: Add `inset` to change shadow from outer to inner (optional).

 You can produce some interesting effects other than shadows with the `box-shadow` property. You can give an element an inner or outer glow by setting the `offset` values to zero and adjusting the blur and spread (see the previous two examples).

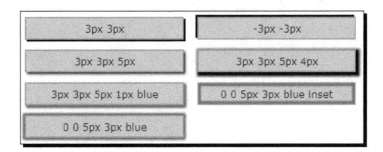

Text shadows

In addition to box shadows, CSS3 has support for text shadows using the `text-shadow` property. It works nearly identically to `box-shadow` and uses almost all the same parameters:

```
text-shadow: h-offset v-offset blur-radius color;
```

Like `box-shadow`, you can produce some interesting effects, such as glowing text:

Time for action – styles in action

Let's put the `border-radius` and `box-shadow` effects to good use in our task list application. First, we will center the task list on the page. Then we'll put a box around each task with rounded corners and a shadow. Let's open `taskAtHand.css` and make some changes. You can find the code for this section in `chapter2/example2.1`.

First, we'll change the style for the `<div id="main">` element which contains the task-name text field and task list. Let's give this section a minimum width of `9em` and a maximum width of `25em`. We don't want the task list to get too wide or too small to make it easier to read. This will give us the beginnings of a reactive layout. We will also set the top and bottom margins to `1em`, and the left and right margins to `auto` to center it on the page.

 A reactive layout is one that reacts to its environment by adjusting its layout to fit the device it is displayed on. By using reactive layouts, you can ensure that your application works and looks good on any device, ranging from a phone to the desktop.

```
#main
{
    max-width: 25em;
    min-width: 9em;
    margin: 1em auto;
}
```

We also want to change the `task-name` text input field to take up the entire width of the main section by setting its `width` property to `98%`. This will give it a little wiggle room for the borders of the textbox; `100%` will make it burst at the seams:

```
#task-name
{
    font-size: 1em;
    display: block;
```

```
        width: 98%;
    }
```

Now let's work on the `task-list` items. We will give them a background color, rounded corners, and a shadow. We will make the shadow black and give it some transparency, so that the background color shows through. We will also set the `position` property to `relative`, so we can position the task buttons inside of it (see the next screenshot):

```
#task-list .task
{
    position: relative;
    list-style: none;
    padding: 0.25em;
    margin: 0.25em;
    background-color: beige;
    border-radius: 4px;
    box-shadow: 2px 2px 3px rgba(0, 0, 0, 0.6);
}
```

Let's also add a border around the task buttons to group them, and move them over to the upper-right side of the `task` element using absolute positioning. We could also float it right here, but absolute positioning gives us more control:

```
#task-list .task .tools
{
    position: absolute;
    top: 0.25em;
    right: 0.25em;
    border: 1px solid black;
    border-radius: 2px;
}
```

 When using absolute positioning, elements are positioned relative to the nearest positioned parent element. In this case, that would be the `task` element. That's why we set its `position` property to `relative`.

What just happened?

If you look at the application in the browser, you will notice how much more natural our task list looks. The shadows really make the task items pop out from the page and give them depth. It makes them the stars of the application. By moving the task buttons over to the right out and of the way, we really make the task names stand out:

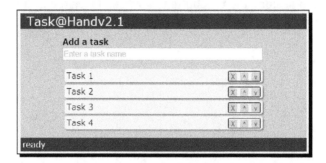

Resize your browser window and see how the list reacts. Here's the same layout resized smaller, like you might see on a phone or some other mobile device:

Backgrounds

There are a number of new styles for setting the background styles of elements. You can now easily draw gradients without using images. You can change the size and origin of background images, and even use multiple images in backgrounds.

Gradients draw a background for an element that fades from one color to one or more other colors. They give depth to your pages and add a more natural look. You can specify two different types of gradients in CSS3: **linear** and **radial**. Linear gradients are, well, linear. They flow from one color to another in a straight line. Radial gradients spread out from a central point in a radial fashion.

Linear gradients

Linear gradients are defined using the linear-gradient specifier on a background property. For the simplest form, you specify a start and end color using any of the color specifiers we discussed earlier in the section on colors, and it will draw the gradient from the top to the bottom of the element. The following fades from red to blue:

```
background: linear-gradient(#FF0000, #0000FF);
```

Although gradients are supported by nearly all browsers at this time, you still have to use browser-specific prefixes to get them to work. That means specifying them at least four times to hit most browsers. Remember to always specify the non-proprietary version last, as shown in the following CSS snippet, so it will override the browser-specific version when available:

```
background: -webkit-linear-gradient(#FF0000, #0000FF);
background: -moz-linear-gradient(#FF0000, #0000FF);
background: -ms-linear-gradient(#FF0000, #0000FF);
background: linear-gradient(#FF0000, #0000FF);
```

If you want the gradient to start somewhere other than the top, you can specify a first parameter that is either the name of the side to start from or the amount to rotate it. The sides are top, bottom, left, and right. You can specify degrees from -360deg to 360deg, or radians from -6.28rad to 6.28rad. 0 is the same as left. A positive number rotates counter clockwise and a negative number clockwise. The following draws a gradient from left to right:

```
background: linear-gradient(left, #FF0000, #0000FF);
```

And the following draws a gradient at 45 degrees, which is from the bottom-left corner:

```
background: linear-gradient(45deg, #FF0000, #0000FF);
```

You may also add more than two color stops if you like. The following draws a gradient at a 45 degree angle from red to blue to green:

```
background: linear-gradient(45deg, #FF0000, #0000FF, #00FF00);
```

Here is how these code snippets will display:

Radial gradients

Radial gradients are nearly identical to linear gradients in the parameters they use. The default is to draw a gradient from the center to the edge of the element:

```
background: radial-gradient(#FF0000, #0000FF);
```

You can also specify a position such as `linear-gradient` using one of the predefined positions or an offset point from the top-left corner for the center of the gradient:

```
background: radial-gradient(top, #FF0000, #0000FF);
```

The following draws the gradient with the center at 20 pixels over and 20 pixels down:

```
background: radial-gradient(20px 20px, #FF0000, #0000FF);
```

You can also add more than two color stops for radial gradients. The following draws the gradient with the center at 20 pixels over and 20 pixels down from red to blue to green:

```
background: radial-gradient(20px 20px, #FF0000, #0000FF, #00FF00);
```

Here is how these code snippets will display:

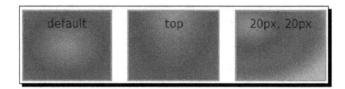

There are many more settings that you can specify for gradients to achieve some interesting effects, but they are beyond the scope of this book. If you find that creating your own gradients is too hard, you can find an excellent gradient generator at `http://www.colorzilla.com/gradient-editor/`.

Background images

You can set the size of a background image to either a fixed pixel amount or a percentage of the area of the element. The image will be scaled to fit in the area specified. The `background-size` property takes two values: a horizontal size and a vertical size. If you want a background image to fill the entire background of an element, you can use the following:

```
background-size: 100% 100%;
```

You can specify multiple background images by separating them with commas. The first image in the list will be drawn on top and the last will be drawn on the bottom. The following draws two background images:

```
background: url(bg-front.png),
            url(bg-back.png);
```

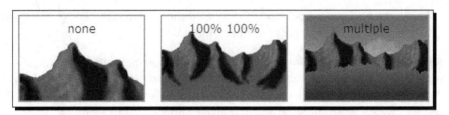

There is also a new `background-origin` property that determines where the background image is drawn. The possible values are as follows:

◆ `content-box`: Draws the background image only in the content area of an element

◆ `padding-box`: Draws the background image out into the padding area of an element

◆ `border-box`: Draws the background image all the way out into the border of an element

Here is an example:

```
background-origin: content-box;
```

And here is the output:

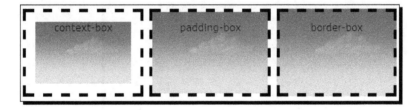

CSS sprites

The next concept we are going to discuss is CSS sprites. This technique isn't new to CSS3, but it is an important thing to know how to use when writing HTML5 applications. CSS sprites allow you to put all of the images for your application in a single image file and then slice the individual images out into elements using CSS. This technique saves the time and network resources required to download multiple images. It is especially useful if your application has a lot of small images.

To implement CSS sprites, put all of your images into a single image file, known as a **sprite sheet**. Then follow these steps to get an image in the sprite sheet into an element on the page:

1. Make the element the same size as the image you want to show.

2. Set the background image of the element to the sprite sheet image.

3. Adjust the background position of the sprite sheet so that the image you want to see is at the top-left corner of the element.

Let's look at an example. The following sprite sheet has 16 images and each image is 10 pixels wide and 10 pixels high. First, we set the element's width and height property to 10 pixels. Next, we set the background image to the sprite-sheet.png sprite sheet. If we were to stop now, we would only get the first image showing in our element.

But we want to show the seventh image in our element. So we need to offset the background position of the sprite sheet by 20 pixels left and 10 pixels up. You must use negative offsets to get the correct image into position because you are moving the background image, not the element:

```
#seven
{
    Width: 10px;
    height: 10px;
    background-image: url(sprite-sheet.png);
    background-position: -20px -10px;
}
```

Here is the result:

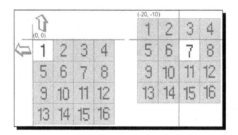

 Think of it as cutting a hole in the web page, then sliding a sprite sheet around behind it until the correct image shows though the hole.

Time for action – adding a gradient and button images

Let's use what we learned about gradients and background images to make our application look more interesting. First, we'll add a gradient to the background of our task list application. We will add a linear gradient to the `<div id="app">` element. It will start with our previous background color at the top and fade into a dark blue color at the bottom. Notice how we keep the old background color as a fallback for browsers that don't support gradients:

```
#app
{
    margin: 4px;
    background-color: #bbc;
    background: -webkit-linear-gradient(top, #bbc, #558);
    background: -moz-linear-gradient(top, #bbc, #558);
    background: -ms-linear-gradient(top, #bbc, #558);
    background: linear-gradient(top, #bbc, #558);
}
```

This is how it would look:

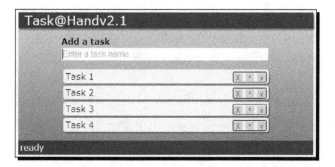

Now let's use CSS sprites to add images to the buttons in our task list application. We need images for delete, move up, and move down. Our buttons will be 16x16 pixels, so our images will need to be the same size. Since we have three images, we will create a sprite sheet that is 48 pixels wide and 16 pixels high. We will put our sprite sheet image file named `icons. png` into the `images` folder.

Now let's open `taskAtHand.css` and add the styling to get the images out of the sprite sheet and into the buttons. First, we will change the style that applies to all the task buttons to set the size to 16x16 pixels and the background image to our sprite sheet. This way, we only have to specify the sprite sheet image once and it will apply to all of our buttons:

```
#task-list .task .tools button
{
    margin: 0;
    padding: 0;
    border: none;
    color: transparent;
    width: 16px;
    height: 16px;
    background: url(images/icons.png);
}
```

Now all of our buttons will use `icons.png` as their background. All we have to do now is set the background positions for each button so they align with the correct image:

```
#task-list .task .tools button.delete
{
    background-position: 0 0;
}
#task-list .task .tools button.move-up
{
    background-position: -16px 0;
}
#task-list .task .tools button.move-down
{
    background-position: -32px 0;
}
```

What just happened?

Take a look at the application in the browser now. We added a gradient so it's not so dull and flat anymore. Now it looks modern and chic. We added images to the buttons using CSS sprites to extract the images from one sprite sheet image. Doesn't this look at lot better with real icons for the buttons?

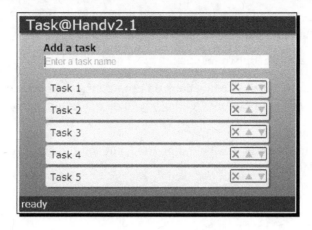

Transitions

We have a pretty good looking UI now, but we can make it even better with some transitions. CSS3 transitions add animation effects to elements when their styles change. For example, if we change the size of an element, it will gradually change from smaller size to a larger size thereby providing visual feedback to the user. When things change gradually, it catches our eye more than something that just appears suddenly on the page.

The CSS3 `transition` property allows us to specify transitions on elements. It has the following format:

```
transition: property duration timing-function delay
```

Here is an explanation of the parameters:

- `property`: The CSS property to add a transition to. For example, `width` or `color`. Use `all` to apply transitions to all the properties.
- `duration`: The length of time the transition takes. For example, `0.5s` takes half a second to complete the transition.
- `timing-function`: Determines how the transition progresses over the duration:
  - `linear`: The same speed from beginning to end
  - `ease`: Starts slow, then speeds up, then ends slow
  - `ease-in`: Starts slow then speeds up
  - `ease-out`: Starts fast then slows down
  - `ease-in-out`: Eases in and then out
  - `cubic-bezier()`: If you don't like the predefined functions, you can build your own
- `delay`: The amount of time to wait before starting the transition.

The `cubic-bezier` function takes four parameters which are numbers from 0 to 1. The following produces the same effect as the `ease` function:

```
transition: all 1s cubic-bezier(0.25, 0.1, 0.25, 1);
```

Building your own `cubic-bezier` functions isn't something most people can just do in their heads. If you want to explore creating your own timing functions, check out `http://cubic-bezier.com/`.

Like the gradients, transitions are widely supported, but you should still use browser-specific prefixes when declaring it:

```
-webkit-transition: all 1s ease;
-moz-transition: all 1s ease;
-o-transition: all  1s ease;
transition: all 1s ease;
```

The easiest way to apply a transition is in combination with a CSS `hover` selector. The following will fade the background color of an element from white to blue in one quarter of a second when the user moves the mouse over it:

```
#some-element
{
    background-color: White;
    transition: all 0.25s ease;
}
#some-element:hover
{
    background-color: Blue;
}
```

Transforms

CSS3 transforms provide even more sophisticated effects. There are 2D and 3D transformations available. We will discuss some of the 2D transformations here. Transforms can be used with transitions to provide some interesting effects. Here is the basic form of the `transform` property:

```
transform: function();
```

There are a few different 2D `transform` functions. The first we'll look at is `translate()`. It moves an element from its current position to a new position. It takes x and y positions as parameters. You can use negative values to move up and to the left. The following would move an element 10 pixels right and 25 pixels up:

```
transform: translate(10px, -25px);
```

The rotate() function rotates an element by a given amount. The rotation amount can be specified in degrees or radians. Use negative values to rotate counter clockwise, positive for clockwise:

```
transform: rotate(45deg);
```

The scale() function adjusts the size of an element by some factor. It takes one or two parameters. If only one parameter is provided, it scales by that amount. If two parameters are specified, it scales the horizontal and vertical axes separately. The following example doubles the width and halves the height of an element:

```
transform: scale(2, 0.5);
```

The last one we'll look at is the skew() function. This function skews, or stretches an element. It takes two parameters which are the amounts to rotate the x and y axes by. Angles are specified the same as the rotate() function:

```
transform: skew(45deg, 10deg);
```

Transformations also require browser-specific prefixes:

```
-webkit-transform: rotate(45deg);
-moz-transform: rotate(45deg);
-o-transform: rotate(45deg);
-ms-transform: rotate(45deg);
transform: rotate(45deg);
```

The following is how transformations would look like in a browser:

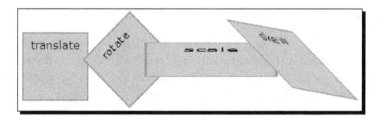

Time for action – effects in action

Let's add some effects to the task list. First, we will add the ability to select a task in the list. When a task is clicked, it will grow in size and get a colored border so it's easy to tell that it is selected. We will also add a hover effect to the tasks so that when the user moves the mouse over a task, the task's action buttons are shown. When the mouse moves off of a task, the buttons will fade back out. You can find the code for this section in chapter2/example2.2.

The first thing we need to do is go back to `taskAtHand.js` and add a `click` event handler to the `task` element after it is created in the `addTaskElement()` method:

```
$task.click(function() { onSelectTask($task); });
```

It calls the `onSelectTask()` method when a task is clicked. In this method we will mark a `task` element as selected by giving it a class name of `selected`. We will also remove the `selected` class from the previously selected task element:

```
function onSelectTask($task)
{
    if ($task)
    {
        // Unselect other tasks
        $task.siblings(".selected").removeClass("selected");
        // Select this task
        $task.addClass("selected");
    }
}
```

Now let's add a style in `taskAtHand.css` for the selected task. We will increase the padding to make the element bigger, add a border to highlight it, and change the background color:

```
#task-list .task.selected
{
    padding: 0.6em 0.5em;
    border: 2px solid orange;
    border-radius: 6px;
    background-color: white;
}
```

That's nice, but we can make it better by adding a transition. We will add the `transition` property to the `.task` class. It will ease in all property changes over one quarter of a second. This will provide some nice visual feedback to the user when they select a task:

```
#task-list .task
{
    /* Not shown... */
    -webkit-transition: all 0.25s ease;
    -moz-transition: all 0.25s ease;
    -o-transition: all 0.25s ease;
    transition: all 0.25s ease;
}
```

While we're at it, let's add one more transition. We will hide the task action buttons until the user moves the mouse over a task or selects a task. To do that, all we need to do is add a little more CSS. First, we will hide the task buttons' container element by setting its `opacity` property to `0` to make it transparent. Then we add the same `transition` properties as we did previously:

```
#task-list .task .tools
{
    position: absolute;
    top: 0.25em;
    right: 0.25em;
    border: 1px solid black;
    border-radius: 2px;
    opacity: 0;

    -webkit-transition: all 0.25s ease;
    -moz-transition: all 0.25s ease;
    -o-transition: all 0.25s ease;
    transition: all 0.25s ease;
}
```

Now we add a `hover` selector for the `task` element that sets the `opacity` property to `1` to make it opaque. This, along with the transition, will make the task buttons appear to fade in when the user hovers over a task. We also add a selector to make the task buttons show up when a task is selected (the second line in the following snippet):

```
#task-list .task:hover .tools,
#task-list .task.selected .tools
{
    opacity: 1;
}
```

Before CSS3, you could do the same thing with JavaScript using the jQuery `fadeIn()` and `fadeOut()` methods along with some mouse events, but it required considerably more code.

What just happened?

We added some CSS3 transitions to the task list to make the task item buttons fade in and out and make selected task items grow larger when clicked. We've seen that with just a few lines of CSS we can add some nice effects to our applications. Here's what our task list looks like now with **Task 2** selected:

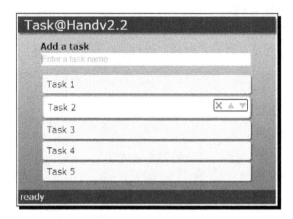

Dynamic stylesheets

Let's add a new feature to our application to allow the user to select a color scheme, or theme, so they can customize the look and feel of the application. We can change the look of a web page by dynamically loading CSS files to override existing styles in our default stylesheet. To implement this, we will add a drop-down list of themes to our application that the user can choose from. When they change the theme, it will change the stylesheet which will change the color of the page.

Time for action – adding a theme selector

To start with, we need a place to put the theme selector. So let's add a toolbar to the task list application's markup in `taskAtHand.html`. We will insert it between the `<header>` and `<div id="main">` elements. The toolbar will contain a `<label>` and a `<select>` drop-down list. The list will contain four different color themes: `blue`, `green`, `magenta`, and `red`. You can find the code for this section in `chapter2/example2.3`:

```
<div id="app">
  <header>Task@Hand</header>
  <div id="toolbar">
    <label for="theme">Theme</label>
    <select id="theme" title="Select theme">
      <option value="blue">Blue</option>
```

```
        <option value="green">Green</option>

        <option value="magenta">Magenta</option>
        <option value="red">Red</option>
        </select>
    </div>
    <div id="main">
```

Now let's style up the toolbar. We will make the font a little smaller than the rest of the page and set the background color as black with some transparency so the color behind it bleeds through:

```
#toolbar
{
    padding: 0.25em;
    font-size: 0.8em;
    color: WhiteSmoke;
    background-color: rgba(0, 0, 0, 0.4);
}
```

Next, we have to implement the different themes. So let's create a few new CSS files, one for each theme. We will put them in a folder named themes to keep them grouped together. The CSS files will have the same names as the <option> values: blue.css, green.css, magenta.css, and red.css. Let's take a look at green.css:

```
#app
{
    background-color: #bcb;
    background: -webkit-linear-gradient(top, #bcb, #585);
    background: -moz-linear-gradient(top, #bcb, #585);
    background: -ms-linear-gradient(top, #bcb, #585);
    background: linear-gradient(top, #bcb, #585);
}
#app>header,
#app>footer
{
    background-color: #060;
}
```

Starting at the top we override the background gradients for the app element to make them a green color instead of blue. We also change the header and footer elements to make them green too. The other CSS files will be exactly the same as this one except they will have different colors.

Now let's add a stylesheet `<link>` element to the `<header>` element of the HTML file for the theme CSS file. Since the blue theme is the default, we will set it to load `blue.css`:

```
<link href="taskAtHand.css" rel="StyleSheet" />
<link id="theme-style" href="themes/blue.css" rel="StyleSheet" />
```

Notice that we include the theme stylesheet after the base one. That's what will allow us to override the default styles. Also note that we give the `<link>` element an ID attribute, so we will be able to get to it in our JavaScript later on.

The rest of the code we need to add is in `taskAtHand.js`. First, we will add a `change` event handler for the theme selector in the `TaskAtHand.start()` method:

```
$("#theme").change(onChangeTheme);
```

When the user chooses a new theme, it will call the `onChangeTheme()` private method:

```
function onChangeTheme()
{
    var theme = $("#theme>option").filter(":selected").val();
    setTheme(theme);
    appStorage.setValue("theme", theme);
}
```

This method gets the selected option from the list by getting its `<option>` elements and then finding the selected option using jQuery's `:selected` selector inside the `filter()` method. Then it calls the `setTheme()` method, which we will implement next. Lastly, we save the selected theme to `localStorage` so we can set it the next time the user comes back to the application.

The `setTheme()` method takes the theme name as a parameter. It gets the `<link id="theme-style">` element and changes its `href` attribute to the new stylesheet's URL:

```
function setTheme(theme)
{
    $("#theme-style").attr("href", "themes/" + theme + ".css");
}
```

When this happens, the page will load the new stylesheet and apply its styles over the existing ones. And just like that, the page changes color.

Wait, we're not done yet. Remember how we saved the theme to `localStorage`? Now we have to get it back out when the user returns to our application. We will create a `loadTheme()` method to do that:

```
function loadTheme()
{
```

```
var theme = appStorage.getValue("theme");
if (theme)
{
    setTheme(theme);
    $("#theme>option[value=" + theme + "]")
        .attr("selected","selected");
}
}
```

This method gets the theme name from `localStorage`. If it finds one, it calls `setTheme()` to set it. Then it selects that theme in the drop-down by finding the `<option>` in the list that has the theme name for its value, and sets the `selected` attribute on it. The final thing to do is add a call to `loadTheme()` from the `start()` method, and we're done.

 The style changes for our theme were pretty simple, but you could completely change the look and feel of your application using this technique.

What just happened?

We added a theme selector that changes the theme stylesheet, which causes the page to use different colors to draw the background. We saved the selected theme to local storage so the settings are remembered when the user returns to the application.

Filling the window

Before we leave the chapter on CSS, there is one more thing we will restyle. Let's make the application so that it fills the entire space of the window. Right now as the list grows, the background gradient grows and the footer moves down. It would be nicer if the gradient covered the entire window and the footer was always at the bottom.

Time for action – expanding the application

We can fill the browser window by using absolute positioning. Let's add the following to the styles for the `<div id="app">` element:

```
#app
{
    position: absolute;
    top: 0;
    bottom: 0;
    left: 0;
    right: 0;
```

```
    overflow: auto;
    /* Code not shown... */
}
```

First, it sets positioning for the element to absolute so that we can set the position of the element to whatever we want. Then we set all of the `position` properties to 0. This stretches the element so that it fills the entire space of the window. Lastly, we set the `overflow` property to `auto`. This will make a scrollbar appear and the gradient extend below the bottom of the window if the list of tasks goes beyond the height of the window.

We also need to reposition the footer so it sticks to the bottom of the window. We can do that the same way, by setting `position` to `absolute` and `bottom` to 0. Notice that we didn't set `right` to 0, so the footer doesn't span the entire width. Otherwise, it might interfere with the task list:

```
#app>footer
{
    position: absolute;
    bottom: 0;
    /* Code not shown... */
}
```

What just happened?

We expanded the main application element to take up the entire space of the browser window and moved the footer to the bottom. Let's see how our app now looks in the browser:

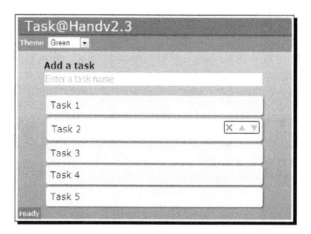

Have a go hero

Think up and implement some more themes. Use some more of the CSS3 features we learned such as radial gradients, background images, or even some box shadows to produce some interesting-looking themes.

Pop quiz

Q1. How many color stops can a gradient have?

1. One
2. Two
3. Three
4. Any number

Q2. What does a transition do?

1. Transitions CSS properties from one value to another
2. Transitions an element from one type into another
3. Transitions from one class to another
4. Transitions from one view to another

Summary

In this chapter, we learned about some of the new CSS3 features that can be used to make your applications pop and provide a lot of visual feedback to the user. We updated our tasklist application by adding rounded corners and shadows to the task elements, and adding images to the task tool buttons. We added a gradient to the background and a theme selector to allow the user to change the color scheme. We also added some transitions to make changes look more natural.

We covered the following concepts in this chapter.

- How to define colors with transparencies in CSS3
- How to give elements rounded corners
- How to add shadows to elements and text
- How to create linear and radial gradients
- How to use CSS3 transitions and transforms to create visual effects
- How to use CSS sprites to reduce the network footprint of your applications
- How to dynamically load stylesheets
- How to make your application fill the entire window

One last thing before we go on. Let me leave you with a word of warning. Just because CSS3 has all of these great effects, it doesn't mean you have to use them all in your application. Every text doesn't need a shadow, you don't need to make your backgrounds have rainbow-colored gradients, and every element doesn't need to be rotated 30 degrees. Judicious use of these effects will make your application look professional; overuse will make them look comical.

In the next chapter, we will take our task list application to the next level by adding a details section to each task that uses some of the new HTML5 input types. We will also learn how to use custom data attributes to bind the data model to input elements.

3

The Devil is in the Details

"Men who wish to know about the world must learn about it in its particular details."

—Heraclitus

This chapter is all about the new HTML5 input types and how to interact with them using JavaScript. In Chapter 1, The Task at Hand, we created a task list application and in Chapter 2, Let's Get Stylish, we styled it using new CSS3 styles. In this chapter we continue to improve it by adding a task details section using the new HTML5 input types. Then we will use custom data attributes to automatically bind values in the view to the data model in our application. We will also add some jQuery animations to make UI transitions smoother.

We will learn the following topics in this chapter:

- The new HTML5 input types and what benefits they provide
- Custom data attributes and their uses
- How to bind a data model to input elements using custom data attributes
- Using jQuery animation methods to hide and show elements
- Using timers to queue up saves to localStorage

HTML5 input types

HTML5 comes with a whole host of new input types. These new types are designed to provide formatting, validation, and in some cases, selectors. For touch devices some of them provide a different set of keys for the keyboard. Not all of the new input types are supported by all browsers yet. Fortunately for us, if a browser doesn't support a type it will just display it as a normal text field. Unfortunately for us, you can't depend on the browser to provide the correct formatted data if the unsupported types are only shown as text fields. So make sure you have a backup plan if you are going to use them.

Here are a few of the more useful new input types with images of the ones that are supported by Chrome.

 See examples in `Chapter 3/input-types/input-types.html`.

Color

The `color` input type is used to choose a color. When clicked it usually displays a color picker. The value is a hex color specifier (for example, #FF0000). This control isn't widely supported for now, so use with caution.

```
<input type="color" value="#FF0000"/>
```

Date

The `date` input type is used to select a date. When clicked it usually displays a date picker. The value is a date string in the format yyyy-mm-dd (for example, 2013-01-23). You may also specify the `min` and `max` attributes in the same date format to limit the date span:

```
<input type="date" value="2013-01-23" min="2013-01-01"/>
```

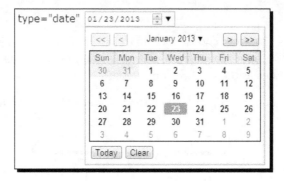

Email

The email input type is used to enter an e-mail address. It looks and behaves like a standard text field. On touch devices the keyboard usually changes to provide e-mail symbols such as the @ sign and *.com*:

```
<input type="email" value="foo@bar.com"/>
```

Number

The number input type is used to enter a number. It is usually displayed with up and down buttons (a spinner control) that change the value by the step amount when clicked. On touch devices the keyboard may change to a number pad. There are a few attributes you can use to restrict the field:

- min: This specifies the minimum value allowed
- max: This specifies the maximum value allowed
- step: This specifies the amount by which value changes when you click on the up or down spinner buttons

```
<input type="number" value="23" min="0" max="100" step="1"/>
```

Range

The range input type is used to choose a value from a range of values. This is nearly identical to the number input type, except that it is usually displayed as a slider control. It has the same attributes as the number input type.

```
<input type="range" value="20" min="0" max="100" step="10"/>
```

Time

The time input type is used to select a time. When clicked it may display a time picker or you can set the time using the spinners. The value is a 24-hour format time string in the format hh:mm:ss (for example, 13:35:15).

```
<input type="time" value="13:35:15"/>
```

URL

The url input type is used to enter a URL. Like the email type, touch devices usually display a keyboard optimized for entering a URL.

```
<input type="url" value="http://www.worldtreesoftware.com"/>
```

Datalist

In addition to these new input types, a new <datalist> form element has been added in HTML5. It is used to add a drop-down list of hints to a text field. When the user starts typing in the text field, all of the list options that match the letters being typed will be shown in a dropdown under the field. The user can select one of the options to automatically fill in the field.

You associate a <datalist> element with a text field by setting an ID on the <datalist> element, and referencing it with the list attribute of an <input> element.

```
<input type="text" list="color-list"/>
<datalist id="color-list">
    <option value="Red"/>
    <option value="Orange"/>
    <option value="Yellow"/>
    <option value="Green"/>
```

```
      <option value="Blue"/>
      <option value="Purple"/>
</datalist>
```

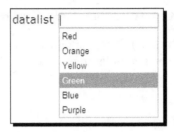

 Because implementation of the new input types is spotty at this times, be cautious when using them. Using a `number` field isn't going to cause many problems if it's not supported; the user can still enter a number in the text field. But something like the `color` field, if not supported, shows as a text field. Will your user be willing to enter a color in hex code in that case?

Autofocus

There's one more useful addition to HTML5 input elements. A new `autofocus` attribute was added to set the focus on a particular `<input>` element when the page is first loaded. Previously we did this in our application by calling the jQuery `focus()` method for the `<input id="new-task-name">` element. We can do the same thing in HTML5 by just adding the `autofocus` attribute.

```
<input type="text" autofocus id="new-task-name".../>
```

Task details

Let's put some of these new input types to good use in our task list application. At the moment all we have is a task name input field. There's not much we can do with that. So let's add some fields to each task to allow the user to define more details about them. You can find the source code for this section in `Chapter 3\example3.1`.

Time for action – adding task details

We will give each task the following new fields:

- **Start date**: The date the task should start. The input type is `date`.
- **Due date**: The date the task should be done by. The input type is `date`.

- ◆ **Status**: Drop-down list `<select>` with options for **None**, **Not Started**, **Started**, and **Completed**.

- ◆ **Priority**: Drop-down list `<select>` with options for **None**, **Low**, **Normal**, and **High**.

- ◆ **% Complete**: The input type is `number`, with a valid range from **0** to **100**.

Let's define these fields in the task template markup in `taskAtHand.html`. The details for each task will be displayed in a section under the task name. Our template now looks like the following code snippet:

```
<li class="task">
    <span class="task-name"></span>
    <input type="text" class="task-name hidden"/>
    <div class="tools">
        <button class="delete" title="Delete">X</button>
        <button class="move-up" title="Up">^</button>
        <button class="move-down" title="Down">v</button>
    </div>
    <div class="details">
        <label>Start date:</label>
        <input type="date"/><br/>
        <label>Due date:</label>
        <input type="date"/><br/>
        <label>Status:</label>
        <select>
            <option value="0">None</option>
            <option value="1">Not Started</option>
            <option value="2">Started</option>
            <option value="3">Completed</option>
        </select><br/>
        <label>Priority:</label>
        <select>
            <option value="0">None</option>
            <option value="1">Low</option>
            <option value="2">Normal</option>
            <option value="3">High</option>
        </select><br/>
        <label>% Complete:</label>
        <input type="number min="0" max="100" step="10" value="0"/>
    </div>
</li>
```

First we added a new `<div class="details">` element to contain the new detail fields. This allows us to separate the details from the task name to style it differently. Then we added the labels and fields to it. Note that for **% Complete** we set the `min` and `max` attributes of the `number` field to limit the number between 0 and 100.

Next we need to style the details section. We will give it a gray background and rounded corners. We make all the labels of same width and align them to right so that all the input fields line up. We then set the `<select>` element of **Status** and **Priority** to a fixed width so they line up as well.

```
#task-list .task .details
{
    display: block;
    background-color: gray;
    color: white;
    border-radius: 4px;
    margin-top: 0.5em;
    padding: 0.25em;
    overflow: auto;
}
#task-list .task .details label
{
    width: 8em;
    text-align: right;
    display: inline-block;
    vertical-align: top;
    font-size: 0.8em;
}
#task-list .task .details select
{
    width: 8em;
}
```

What just happened?

We added a task details section to our tasks using some of the new HTML5 input types. The following screenshot shows what the task item looks like now with a details section:

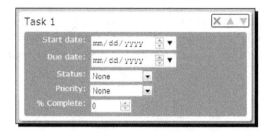

Time for action – hiding task details

This looks good, but it's also taking up a lot of room. If each task in the list is this long it will soon scroll off the page and we won't be able to see an overview of the task list very well. Since the task details are optional fields anyway, we can make our list more compact by not showing the details until the user wants to see them. We'll do that by hiding the details section and adding a toggle button next to the task name to show or hide the details when clicked.

First let's add the toggle details button next to the task name in our task template and give it a class named `toggle-details`:

```
<li class="task">
    <button class="toggle-details">+</button>
    <span class="task-name"></span>
    <!-- Not shown… -->
</li>
```

Now let's implement the toggle button in our JavaScript code. First we add a click event handler for the toggle button in the `addTaskElement()` method that calls the `toggleDetails()` method:

```
$("button.toggle-details", $task).click(function() {
    toggleDetails($task);
});
```

Then we implement the `toggleDetails()` method:

```
function toggleDetails($task)
{
    $(".details", $task).slideToggle();
    $("button.toggle-details", $task).toggleClass("expanded");
}
```

The `toggleDetails()` method uses a couple of new jQuery methods that we haven't seen yet. It toggles the visibility of the task details using `slideToggle()` and toggles the `expanded` class on the button using `toggleClass()`. The `toggleClass()` method adds a class to an element if the element doesn't already have it, and removes it if it does.

The `slideToggle()` method is an animation function that toggles the visibility of an element. It makes an element visible using a sliding down motion pushing the elements below it down. To hide the element it slides it back up, shrinking it until it's hidden. There is also a method to fade elements in and out called `fadeToggle()`. But a slide provides a smoother transition when an element moves other elements out of the way when it becomes visible.

 In general a slide looks better when the element pushes the elements below it down when it's made visible. It is also good for menu-like behavior. A fade usually looks best when you are making an element visible that displays over the top of other elements.

Now let's add some styling to the button. Of course we want some nice icons like our other task buttons, so let's add them to our sprite sheet file, `icons.png`. We need an image to show when the task properties are collapsed and one to show when they are expanded. Let's create a second row of images for these two icons.

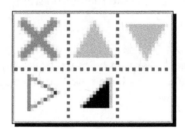

The first thing we need to do back in our stylesheet is set `display` to `none` for the details so that they are hidden by default:

```
#task-list .task .details
{
    display: none;
    /* Not shown... */
}
```

Then we add styles for the `toggle-details` button. As we are using the same sprite sheet as the task tools buttons, we'll use the same style for our new button by adding it to the CSS selector. Then we'll add selectors to get the images into the button using background position offsets:

```
#task-list .task .tools button,
#task-list .task button.toggle-details
{
    /* Not shown… */
    background: url(images/icons.png);
}
#task-list .task button.toggle-details
{
    background-position: 0 -16px;
}
#task-list .task button.toggle-details.expanded
{
    background-position: -16px -16px;
}
```

The vertical offset for our `toggle-details` images is `-16px` because they are on the second row in the sprite sheet. Notice that the second image matches to the `expanded` class. We are adding the `expanded` class to the button when details are visible.

What just happened?

We added a toggle button to each task that hides or shows the task details when clicked. Open it in the browser and see what we have now. You can open and close task details and they smoothly slide open and closed. Pretty cool.

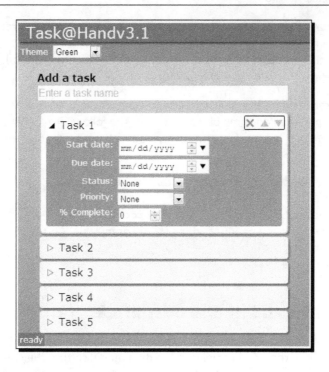

Custom data attributes

Another new feature of HTML5 is custom data attributes. Custom data attributes allow you to store custom data private to your application as an attribute on any element in the DOM. All you have to do is prefix the attribute name with `data-`. The name should be all lower case letters. You can assign any string value to the attribute.

For example, say we had a list of products and we wanted to store information about the products, such as product ID and category. All we have to do is add `data-product-id` and `data-category` attributes to the associated elements:

```html
<ul id="product-list">
  <li data-product-id="d1e0ddde" data-category="widgets">
    Basic Widget
  </li>
  <li data-product-id="e6b2c03f" data-category="widgets">
    Super Widget
  </li>
</ul>
```

So now that we have custom attributes, we can extract the custom data from the elements using JavaScript and use it in our applications. jQuery happens to have a `data()` method designed just for this purpose. You give it the name of the custom attribute, minus the `data-`, and it returns the value associated with it.

Continuing with the previous example, let's say we want to allow the user to click on a product in the list and then do some processing on it. The following `setSelectedProduct()` method uses the `data()` method to extract the product ID and category from the element that was clicked:

```
$("#product-list li").click(function() {
    var $product = $(this);
    var productId = $product.data("product-id");
    var category = $product.data("category");
    // Do something...
});
```

Data binding with custom attributes

A great use for custom data attributes is to implement data binding. Data binding allows us to map user controls in the DOM to fields in the data model so that they are automatically updated when the user changes them. Using this technique we can eliminate a lot of boring repetitive code that does nothing more than handle events and map fields in the view to fields in the model.

 There are a few excellent data binding libraries available for JavaScript, including `Backbone.js` and `Knockout`. We will implement our own simple data binding here to learn how to use custom attributes. If you find yourself building an application with a lot of data you might consider using one of these libraries.

Time for action – building a data model

Before we can begin implementing data binding, we need a data model to bind to. If you recall, we are only saving the task names to `localStorage`. Our data model is simply an array of strings. Now that each task has multiple details fields we will need something a little more substantial to hold all of that data. You can find the source code for this section in `Chapter 3\example3.2`.

Let's start by defining a task object for our data model. We will create a new file, `taskList.js` to put it in:

```
function Task(name)
```

Chapter 3

```
{
    this.name = name;
    this.id = Task.nextTaskId++;
    this.created = new Date();
    this.priority = Task.priorities.normal;
    this.status = Task.statuses.notStarted;
    this.pctComplete = 0;
    this.startDate = null;
    this.dueDate = null;
}
// Define some "static variables" on the Task object
Task.nextTaskId = 1;
Task.priorities = {
    none: 0,
    low: 1,
    normal: 2,
    high: 3
};
Task.statuses = {
    none: 0,
    notStarted: 1,
    started: 2,
    completed: 3
};
```

Starting from the top, our constructor takes one parameter-the task name. It uses that to set the name field in the object. Each task has a unique task ID, which gets incremented every time a task is created. The rest of the members are set to default values.

We are attaching a `Task.nextTaskId` field to the `Task` object constructor to keep track of what the next unique task ID should be. Doing this allows us to define what we would call static or class variables in languages that have classes, such as Java or C# (where they are defined using static variables). The `nextTaskId` field will get saved to `localStorage` whenever it changes so that we know where we left off when the user returns to the application.

Notice that `priority` and `status` are using enumerations. We implement those as static objects (because JavaScript doesn't have enumerations) attached to the `Task` constructor.

The next thing we need is a list to store the `Task` objects in. To make it easier to manage the code for this, we will create a `TaskList` object that is basically a wrapper over an array. It provides methods to add, remove, and get tasks:

```
function TaskList(tasks)
{
    tasks = tasks || [];
```

The constructor takes one optional parameter that is an array of the `Task` objects. The first line of the constructor checks to see if an array was passed in. If not, it creates a new empty array using empty square brackets (`[]`).

 In JavaScript the logical OR operator (`||`) can act as a null-coalescing operator. It returns the left-hand operand if the operand is "truthy"; otherwise it returns the right operand. In this case, truthy means that a `tasks` parameter was passed in and is not `null` or `undefined`. This is very useful paradigm for defining default values.

Now we add a public `getTasks()` method that simply returns the array. We will need access to it later to save the tasks:

```
this.getTasks = function()
{
    return tasks;
};
```

Next we add a public `addTask()` method that takes a `Task` object and appends it to the end of the array:

```
this.addTask = function(task)
{
    tasks.push(task);
    return this;
};
```

The public `removeTask()` method takes a task ID as a parameter and removes the associated task from the list:

```
this.removeTask = function(taskId)
{
    var i = getTaskIndex(taskId);
    if (i >= 0)
    {
        var task = tasks[i];
        tasks.splice(i, 1);
        return task;
    }
    return null;
};
```

It gets the index of the task by calling `getTaskIndex()`, then uses the `array.splice()` method to remove it from the `tasks` array. The `getTaskIndex()` method is a private method that takes a task ID as a parameter and searches through the array to find the task with that ID. If it finds the task it returns it. Otherwise it returns `-1`:

```
function getTaskIndex(taskId)
{
    for (var i in tasks)
    {
        if (tasks[i].id == taskId)
        {
            return parseInt(i);
        }
    }
    // Not found
    return -1;
}
```

Next up is the public `getTask()` method. It takes a task ID as a parameter and also uses the `getTaskIndex()` method to find it. It returns the associated `Task` object, or `null` if it doesn't exist.

```
this.getTask = function(taskId)
{
    var index = getTaskIndex(taskId);
    return (index >= 0 ? tasks[index] : null);
};
```

The last public method we are going to add is called `each()`. It takes a reference to a `callback` function as a parameter. It loops over the array of tasks and executes the `callback` function for each task in the array. This method can be used to iterate over all tasks in the list:

```
this.each = function(callback)
{
    for (var i in tasks)
    {
        callback(tasks[i]);
    }
};
}
```

Time for action – implementing the bindings

Let's head back over to the task template in our HTML file and add some custom data attributes. We'll add custom attributes to all of the task details `<input>` and `<select>` elements. The data attribute name will be `data-field`, and the attribute value will be the name of the field the element matches to in the `Task` object. We will use those attributes later in our JavaScript to hook the DOM elements and data model together:

```
<div class="details">
    <label>Start date:</label>
    <input type="date" data-field="startDate"/><br/>
    <label>Due date:</label>
    <input type="date" data-field="dueDate"/><br/>
    <label>Status:</label>
    <select data-field="status">
        <!- options removed... -->
    </select><br/>
    <label>Priority:</label>
    <select data-field="priority">
        <!- options removed... -->
    </select><br/>
    <label>% Complete:</label>
    <input type="number" data-field="pctComplete"
        min="0" max="100" step="10" value="0"/>
</div>
```

Now that we have a data model, we need to go into the `TaskAtHandApp` object in `taskAtHand.js` and update it to use that model. First we'll add a `taskList` variable and initialize it to an instance of a `TaskList` object:

```
function TaskAtHandApp()
{
    var version = "v3.2",
        appStorage = new AppStorage("taskAtHand"),
        taskList = new TaskList();
```

Then we'll go into the `addTask()` method and add code to create a new `Task` object, and add it to the task list. This is also where we save the `nextTaskId` value into `localStorage` after it's been incremented:

```
function addTask()
{
    var taskName = $("#new-task-name").val();
    if (taskName)
    {
        var task = new Task(taskName);
```

```
            taskList.addTask(task);
            appStorage.setValue("nextTaskId", Task.nextTaskId);
            addTaskElement(task);
            saveTaskList();
            // Reset the field
            $("#new-task-name").val("").focus();
        }
    }
```

Notice that we also changed the parameter of the addTaskElement() method to pass in the Task object. So let's update the addTaskElement() method to take a Task object as the parameter instead of a task name:

```
function addTaskElement(task)
{
    var $task = $("#task-template .task").clone();
    $task.data("task-id", task.id);
    $("span.task-name", $task).text(task.name);
```

After creating a new task element in the DOM we set the task ID on it using a custom data attribute named task-id. This is done with the jQuery data() method that takes the data attribute name and value as parameters. Next we set the task name into the <span> attribute from the task.name field.

Now we will implement the first part of the data binding. This next block of code uses the data attributes we previously added to the markup to set the values from the Task object into the associated <input> and <select> elements in the details section:

```
        // Populate all of the details fields
        $(".details input, .details select", $task).each(function() {
            var $input = $(this);
            var fieldName = $input.data("field");
            $input.val(task[fieldName]);
        });
```

Here's how it works:

1. First it finds all <input> and <select> elements inside the task element.

2. Then it calls the jQuery each() method, which is used to iterate over the set of selected elements, passing in a callback function.

3. Inside the callback function this points to the current element. So first we wrap the element in a jQuery object.

4. Then we use the `data()` method to get the value of the `data-field` custom attribute, which is the name of the field in the `Task` object associated with the element.

5. Finally we set the value of the user control to the value of the field in the `Task` object. We get the value from the `Task` object using square brackets. Remember that in JavaScript `object["field"]` is the .same as `object.field`.

 You can think of using square brackets to access object fields as similar to using reflection in C# or Java to dynamically access values in objects at runtime.

Now we need to add code to go the other way. Whenever the user changes the value of a form control we want to automatically save it back to the data model. So let's add a change event handler for each of the details form controls:

```
$(".details input, .details select", $task).change(function() {
    onChangeTaskDetails(task.id, $(this));
});
```

This calls the `onChangeTaskDetails()` method, passing in the task ID and the form control element that changed wrapped in a jQuery object. Let's implement that method:

```
function onChangeTaskDetails(taskId, $input)
{
    var task = taskList.getTask(taskId)
    if (task)
    {
        var fieldName = $input.data("field");
        task[fieldName] = $input.val();
        saveTaskList();
    }
}
```

Let's break it down to see how it works:

1. First it gets the `Task` object from the task list with the specified ID.

2. After making sure we got an object back (you never know, so always check) we get the `Task` object field name from the element's `data-field` attribute.

3. Then we set the value of the field on the `Task` object to the value of the form control element, again using square brackets to access it dynamically.

4. Finally we call `saveTaskList()` to commit the change to `localStorage`.

That reminds me, we need to rewrite the `saveTaskList()` method to save our new `TaskList` object. That's easy enough. We just call the `getTasks()` method of the task list to get the array of `Task` objects. Then we save the array to `localStorage`:

```
function saveTaskList()
{
    appStorage.setValue("taskList", taskList.getTasks());
}
```

 If you have old task list data from the previous examples you will need to delete it before using the new data model. In Chrome developer tools you can click on the item and press the *Delete* key to remove it.

What just happened?

First we created a data model to hold all of the task data. Then we added data binding to our application using custom data attributes to automatically update the data model when a field on the page changes. Then we saved the task list to local storage.

Time for action – loading the task list

Now that we've saved the new data model to `localStorage` we need to update the `loadTaskList()` method to load the data:

```
function loadTaskList()
{
    var tasks = appStorage.getValue("taskList");
    taskList = new TaskList(tasks);
    rebuildTaskList();
}
```

First we get the task array from `localStorage` and pass that as a parameter into the `TaskList` object's constructor. Then we call a new method, `rebuildTaskList()` to create the task elements in the DOM:

```
function rebuildTaskList()
{
    // Remove any old task elements
    $("#task-list").empty();
    // Create DOM elements for each task
    taskList.each(function(task)
    {
        addTaskElement(task);
    });
}
```

First we remove any old elements from the task list element using the jQuery `empty()` method. Then we use the `each()` method that we implemented in the `TaskList` object to iterate over the tasks and call `addTaskElement()` for each one to build the task elements.

Queuing up changes

Now we've bound the user controls to the data model and automatically save it every time a change is made. There's one problem with this though. Input controls like the `number` or `time` types that have spinners associated with them cause a `change` event every time a spinner button is clicked. If the user holds a spinner button down it will fire `change` events at an alarming rate. This will in turn save the task list to `localStorage` repeatedly in a very short period of time. That doesn't seem like a very efficient thing to do, especially if you have a lot of data.

Time for action – delaying the saves

 See the code in `Chapter 3\example3.3`.

We can alleviate this problem by delaying the save to `localStorage` for a period of time to wait until all of the user interaction has finished. This is pretty easy to implement using JavaScript's `setTimeout()` function. We will make this change in the `saveTaskList()` method, but first we need a global variable in the `TaskAtHandApp` object to keep track of the timeout ID returned by `setTimeout()`:

```
function TaskAtHandApp()
{
    var version = "v3.3",
        appStorage = new AppStorage("taskAtHand"),
        taskList = new TaskList(),
        timeoutId = 0;
```

When changes are pending a save, we want to display a message in the status element at the bottom of the page so the user knows that their changes will be saved. When the actual save has taken place we will update the message and fade it out so the user knows the save is complete. To do that we need to rewrite the `setStatus()` method as well:

```
function setStatus(msg, noFade)
{
    $("#app>footer").text(msg).show();
    if (!noFade)
    {
```

```
            $("#app>footer").fadeOut(1000);
        }
    }
```

We add an optional noFade parameter. When set to true the message will not fade out. Otherwise we use the jQuery fadeOut() method to gradually fade out the message over 1000 milliseconds, or one second. Now let's update the saveTaskList() method:

```
function saveTaskList()
{
    if (timeoutId) clearTimeout(timeoutId);
    setStatus("saving changes...", true);
    timeoutId = setTimeout(function()
    {
        appStorage.setValue("taskList", taskList.getTasks());
        timeoutId = 0;
        setStatus("changes saved.");
    },
    2000);
}
```

The first thing we do is check to see if there is already a save pending by checking if the timeoutId variable has a value. If it does, we will cancel the timeout using JavaScript's clearTimeout() function. This has the effect of resetting the timer if the user makes another change while a save is pending. All changes will effectively be queued up and saved at one time.

Next we set a new timeout using setTimeout(). The setTimeout() function takes a function to execute and the number of milliseconds to wait until it executes the function. It returns a timeout ID that we store in our timeoutId variable in case we need to cancel the timeout later.

After 2000 milliseconds, or two seconds of inactivity the task list will be saved. Then we reset the timeoutId variable because our timeout is finished. Finally we call setStatus() to tell the user the changes have been saved.

What just happened?

We used the JavaScript setTimeout() function to effectively queue up changes so we aren't constantly saving the task list when values are changing rapidly.

Have a go hero

That's it; our task list application is complete, as far as this book goes anyway. Now go and add your own features to make it even better. For example, add more task fields such as a text area to enter notes. Maybe add an option to the toolbar to hide completed tasks. Try adding a sorting option to sort the list by name, status, or date.

Pop quiz

Q1. What happens if a browser doesn't support one of the new HTML5 input types?

1.   The input field is not displayed.
2.   The field is displayed as a text field.
3.   The field is set to read only.
4.   The browser shows an error message.

Q2. What kind of element can custom data attributes be used on?

1.   Only form input elements.
2.   Only block level elements.
3.   Only inline elements.
4.   Any element.

Summary

In this chapter we looked at some of the more useful HTML5 input types. We used those input types to create a collapsible task details section for each task. Then we used custom data attributes to implement a simple data binding to map the input fields in the view to the data model.

We covered the following concepts in this chapter:

◆   How and when to use the new HTML5 input types
◆   How to use custom data attributes to store private data in the DOM
◆   How to implement data binding using custom data attributes to bind a data model to form controls
◆   How to use jQuery animation methods to hide and show elements
◆   How to use a timer to delay saves to `localStorage` to make applications more responsive

In the next chapter we will head off in a completely new direction. We'll take a look at the HTML5 canvas element and API and write a brand new application that uses it.

4
A Blank Canvas

"It's so fine and yet so terrible to stand in front of a blank canvas."

—Paul Cezanne

In this chapter we are heading out in a whole new direction. We will learn how to use the new HTML5 canvas element and API by creating a simple drawing application. Our application will use the canvas basics such as strokes, paths, lines, and shapes. We will create a toolbar using custom data attributes, which we learned in the previous chapter, to bind menu items to actions in our code.

We will learn the following in this chapter:

- ◆ The canvas element and its drawing API
- ◆ How to get a canvas context and what are its global properties
- ◆ How to draw lines, rectangles, and other shapes
- ◆ How to get the position of the mouse inside a canvas element
- ◆ How to create a toolbar that contains drop-down menus
- ◆ How to use custom data attributes to bind toolbar actions to JavaScript code

HTML5 canvas

Probably one of the most exciting new features of HTML5 is the canvas. You can use it to create drawings anywhere on a web page. The only way to do this previously was by using some other technology such as Flash, SVG, or some other browser plugin.

The HTML5 canvas is both an element and an API. The `<canvas>` element defines a rectangular area of a web page where graphics can be drawn. The canvas API works with a `<canvas>` element to provide the JavaScript interface to draw on the canvas. It is a low-level set of functions for drawing lines, rectangle, circles, and other graphic primitives.

The `<canvas>` element itself is very simple. You must set the `width` and `height` attributes to specify its size. You can optionally put content inside the `<canvas>` element to be displayed for browsers that don't support it. The good news is that the HTML5 `<canvas>` element is widely supported by nearly every modern browser. The following code creates a canvas element 600 pixels wide and 400 pixels high:

```
<canvas width="600" height="400">
   Sorry, your browser doesn't support canvas.
</canvas>
```

If you set the width and height of a `<canvas>` element in CSS to something other than the size specified on the element, it will stretch or shrink the drawing in the canvas to fit, which may compromise on the image quality.

Getting a context

The canvas API is accessed via a canvas context object. You get the context by calling the `getContext()` method of the `<canvas>` element, passing in a string parameter that defines the type of the context you want:

```
var context = $("canvas")[0].getContext("2d");
```

The only valid context type parameter you can pass into `getContext()` at this time is `"2d"`. This begs the question, "Is there a 3D context?" The answer is *no*, there is not. But we can always hope for one in the future.

Canvas basics

In this section we will learn some of the basics of using the canvas API. Now that we have a context, we can call its methods to draw lines and shapes. The API has a whole host of methods that let you draw everything from the most basic lines, to shapes, and even bitmap images.

You can find the source code for this section in `chapter4/canvas-examples/canvas-examples.html`.

Clearing the canvas

The background of the canvas is transparent. Whatever background color you specify for the canvas element in your CSS will show through. You can clear the canvas, or a portion of it, using the context's `clearRect()` method. It takes *x*, *y*, width, and height parameters and clears that part of the canvas.

```
context.clearRect(0, 0, canvas.width, canvas.height);
```

Context properties

By default, when you draw on the canvas, lines are one pixel wide and the color is black. You can change these by setting global properties on the `context` object.

- `penWidth`: This property sets the width that lines will be drawn with. It can be any decimal number. For example, you can have a line that is 1.5 pixels wide.

- `strokeStyle`: This property sets the color that will be used to draw lines. It can be any one of the CSS color specifiers. For example, to draw in red you could use `red` or `#FF0000`, `rgb(255, 0, 0)`, or `rgba(255, 0, 0, 1)`.

- `fillStyle`: This property sets the color that will be used to fill shapes. Like `strokeStyle` it can be any CSS color specifier.

- `globalAlpha`: This property sets the alpha or transparency amount to draw with. It can be any number from 0 to 1, where 0 is completely transparent and 1 is completely opaque.

- `lineCap`: This property determines how the ends of lines are drawn. It can be one of the following:
  - `butt` draws a flat end
  - `round` draws a rounded end
  - `square` draws a square end

  `square` looks similar to `butt` except that it has an extra rectangle drawn at the end, making it longer.

◆ `lineJoin`: This property determines how corners are drawn where two lines meet. It can be one of the following:

  ❑ `bevel` draws a beveled or flat corner

  ❑ `round` draws a rounded corner

  ❑ `miter` draws a sharp corner

Canvas pad

Now that we know the basics of the canvas API, let's use our newfound knowledge to create a drawing application called **canvas pad**. We'll start off with an application that draws black lines, like drawing with a pen on paper. Then we will add a toolbar and menus so that the user can change options such as width, opacity, color, and select different drawing tools.

Time for action – creating a canvas pad

You can find the source code for this section at `chapter4/example4.1`. Let's start by copying our application template that we created in the first chapter and renaming the file names to `canvasPad.html`, `canvasPad.css`, and `canvasPad.js`. Then we'll go in and change the links in the HTML for those files. Finally we change the main application object in the JavaScript to `CanvasPadApp`.

Now let's add a `<canvas>` element to the HTML right inside the `<div id="main">` element and size it to 600 by 400:

```
<div id="main">
  <canvas width="600" height="400">
    Sorry, your browser doesn't support canvas.
  </canvas>
</div>
```

Next we'll add some styles to the CSS to center the canvas on the page and give it a white background. We'll also use a `box-shadow` element to make it stand out:

```
#main
{
    text-align: center;
```

```
    }
#main>canvas
{
    cursor: crosshair;
    margin: 1em auto;
    background-color: white;
    box-shadow: 0 0 8px 2px #555;
}
```

In order to encapsulate our interaction with the canvas we are going to create a new object called Canvas2D and put it in a file named canvas2d.js. In this object we will create some higher level drawing functions. This object's constructor takes a <canvas> element wrapped in a jQuery object as a parameter:

```
function Canvas2D($canvas)
{
    var context = $canvas[0].getContext("2d"),
        width = $canvas[0].width,
        height = $canvas[0].height;
}
```

The first thing the constructor does is set some private variables. We get the context, width, and height from the $canvas jQuery object.

 You can get access to the underlying element that a jQuery object wraps by using square brackets such as an array. So in this case $canvas[0] gives us the first (and only) <canvas> element.

What just happened?

We created a new canvas pad application from our template and added a canvas to it. We centered the canvas on the page and gave it an all-over shadow to frame it and make it appear to float on top of the page. Finally, we created a Canvas2D object to encapsulate interaction with the canvas.

Time for action – showing the coordinates

The first thing we will implement in our Canvas2D object is a way to convert page coordinates to canvas coordinates. Then we will use that to show the mouse coordinates on the page as the user moves their mouse over the canvas.

The problem with mouse coordinates is that they are always offset from the top left of the web page. To get the canvas coordinates we need to find the offset of the <canvas> element on the page and subtract it from the page coordinates.

First we need a variable named `pageOffset` to hold the offset of the canvas element. We'll set its value using jQuery's `offset()` method, which gets the page offset of an element. It returns an object with `left` and `top` fields:

```
var pageOffset = $canvas.offset();
```

Now we add a `getCanvasPoint()` method. It takes the `pageX` and `pageY` parameters, subtracts the canvas element offsets, and returns a new object with `x` and `y` fields to hold the adjusted coordinates:

```
this.getCanvasPoint = function(pageX, pageY)
{
    return {
        x: pageX - pageOffset.left,
        y: pageY - pageOffset.top
    }
};
```

Since our canvas is centered on the page, whenever the size of the window changes the offset of the canvas will change as well. So we need to add a `resize` event handler to the window so that whenever it changes the `pageOffset` variable gets updated:

```
$(window).resize(function() { pageOffset = $canvas.offset(); });
```

Now let's add the code to show the mouse coordinates in the status bar when the user moves the mouse over the canvas. First we need an instance of the `Canvas2D` object in our application's main class, `CanvasPadApp`. We will assign it to a private variable named `canvas2d`:

```
function CanvasPadApp()
{
    var version = "4.1",
        canvas2d = new Canvas2D($("#main>canvas"));
    // ...
```

We will show the coordinates in the `<footer>` element below the canvas. Let's add a `<span>` in the footer to hold the coordinates:

```
<footer>
  <span id="coords">0, 0</span>
</footer>
```

Next we add a `mousemove` event handler to the `<canvas>` element in the `start()` method. It will call `onMouseMove` when the mouse is moved:

```
this.start = function()
{
    $("#app header").append(version);
```

```
        $("#main>canvas").mousemove(onMouseMove);

    }
```

The onMouseMove event handler calls the canvas2d.getCanvasPoint() method passing in the page coordinates from the mouse event. It gets back the position of the mouse on the canvas and passes that into the showCoordinates() method to display them in the footer:

```
    function onMouseMove(e)
    {
        var canvasPoint = canvas2d.getCanvasPoint(e.pageX, e.pageY);
        showCoordinates(canvasPoint);
    }
    function showCoordinates(point)
    {
        $("#coords").text(point.x + ", " + point.y);
    }
```

The showCoordinates() method uses jQuery's text() method to put the coordinates into the footer. Now if you move the mouse over the canvas on the page you will see the coordinates change. When you move the mouse to the top-left corner it should display **(0, 0)**.

What just happened?

We computed the page offset of the mouse on the canvas by subtracting the position of the canvas from the mouse coordinates. Then we added a mousemove event handler to display the coordinates in the footer when the user moves the mouse over the canvas.

Drawing lines

The first thing we want to implement is a way for the user to draw simple lines, or to scribble on the canvas. To do that we need to get the points when the user moves the mouse with the mouse button pressed down and draw lines between them. So let's learn how to draw on the canvas.

Paths and strokes

The most primitive way to draw on the canvas is by defining paths and then stroking, or drawing them. Think of it as planning what you are going to draw in your head, then putting your pen to the paper, and actually drawing it out.

To create a path you define it by specifying two or more points using moveTo() and lineTo() methods. Then you draw it to the canvas by calling the stroke() method. There are four basic methods that you use to define and draw paths.

- beginPath(): This method starts a new path.

- moveTo(x, y): This method moves the pen to a new position without drawing.

- lineTo(x, y): This method draws a line from the previous position to a new position.

- stroke():This method draws the path onto the canvas. It is important to note that nothing actually gets drawn to the canvas until you call stroke().

The following code draws a line from the point (10, 10) to (80, 100):

```
context.beginPath();
context.moveTo(10, 10);
context.lineTo(80, 100);
context.stroke();
```

You can make any number of calls to the moveTo() and lineTo() methods between beginPath() and stroke(). This allows you to queue up a number of drawing commands and then commit them to the canvas all at once. If you want your path to form a closed shape you can call the closePath() method to draw a line from the last point to the first point. For example, the following code draws a triangle:

```
context.beginPath();
context.moveTo(100, 10);
context.lineTo(150, 90);
context.lineTo(200, 20);
context.closePath();
context.stroke();
```

It's also possible to fill your shapes by calling the context's fill() method instead of stroke(). Actually you can call both fill() and stroke() if you want the shape to be outlined in one color and filled with another:

```
context.beginPath();
context.moveTo(100, 10);
context.lineTo(150, 90);
context.lineTo(200, 20);
context.closePath();
context.fill();
context.stroke();
```

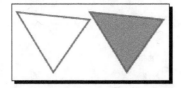

Time for action – using the mouse to draw

The first thing we need to do is capture mouse events. Let's go into our `CanvasPadApp` object and add the code to check for them in the `start()` method. As you may recall, we already added a `mousemove` event handler above. Now we will add handlers for `mousedown`, `mouseup`, and `mouseout` events:

```
$("#main>canvas").mousemove(onMouseMove)
    .mousedown(onMouseDown)
    .mouseup(onMouseUp)
    .mouseout(onMouseUp);
```

No, there's not a mistake in `mouseout`. We want the `mouseout` event to be handled the same way as `mouseup`, so they both stop the drawing process. The `mouseout` event is fired when the mouse leaves the `<canvas>` element. When that happens we can't get `mousemove` events anymore and therefore lose track of the pen position.

Before we implement the event handlers we need a couple of new variables to keep track of things. We need a Boolean value to keep track of when we are drawing, an array to keep track of the current set of points, and an array to keep track of all the sets of points (we will call them actions):

```
var version = "4.1",
canvas2d = new Canvas2D($("#main>canvas")),
drawing = false,
    points = [],
    actions = [];
```

> Note that if you give your global object variables default values it will make it easier for code editors that have an autocomplete feature to figure out what the type of the variable is and give you the appropriate suggestions.

First let's implement `onMouseDown()` since this starts the drawing process. It takes one parameter, which is the mouse event object:

```
function onMouseDown(e)
{
```

```
    e.preventDefault();
        penDown(e.pageX, e.pageY);
    }
    function penDown(pageX, pageY)
    {
        drawing = true;
        points = [];
        points.push(canvas2d.getCanvasPoint(pageX, pageY));
        actions.push(points);
    }
```

The first thing we do in the onMouseDown() method is call preventDefault() on the mouse event object. This will stop the system from doing the default mouse down behavior, part of which is to change the mouse cursor icon. We want it to remain a cross icon, which we previously set in the CSS. Then we call penDown() passing in the page coordinates of the mouse which we get from the mouse event.

In the penDown() method we initialize the drawing process. First, we set the drawing flag to true. Then we create a new array to put the current drawing points into it. Then we add the first point to the array after converting it from page coordinates to canvas coordinates by calling getCanvasPoint(). The final thing we do is add the current points array to the actions array.

The next step in the drawing process is to handle mousemove events, so let's rewrite the onMouseMove() method:

```
    function onMouseMove(e)
    {
        penMoved(e.pageX, e.pageY);
    }
    function penMoved(pageX, pageY)
    {
        var canvasPoint = canvas2d.getCanvasPoint(pageX, pageY);
        showCoordinates(canvasPoint);

        if (drawing)
        {
            points.push(canvasPoint);
            redraw();
        }
    }
```

Now onMouseMove() calls penMoved() passing it the mouse coordinates. The penMoved() method first converts the coordinates then calls showCoordinates() as it did before. Then we check if the drawing flag is set. This was set in the penDown() method so we know that the mouse button is down. If the user is drawing then we add the current point to the array of points and call redraw(), which we will implement next:

```
function redraw()
{
    canvas2d.clear();
    for (var i in actions)
    {
        canvas2d.drawPoints(actions[i]);
    }
}
```

The redraw() method first clears the canvas by calling canvas2d.clear(), which we will write next, then it iterates over all of the actions and calls drawPoints() passing in the set of points for each action.

Now let's go into our Canvas2D object and add the clear() and drawPoints() methods. First, our clear() method calls the context.clearRect() method passing in the canvas width and height variables we defined in the Canvas2D constructor:

```
this.clear = function()
{
    context.clearRect(0, 0, width, height);
    return this;
};
```

Next, the drawPoints() method takes an array of points and draws lines between them:

```
this.drawPoints = function(points)
{
    context.beginPath();
    context.moveTo(points[0].x, points[0].y);
    for (var i = 1; i < points.length; i++)
    {
        context.lineTo(points[i].x, points[i].y);
    }
    context.stroke();
    return this;
};
```

After beginning a new path it calls `moveTo()` to move the pen to the first point in the array. Then it iterates over the remaining points in the array calling `lineTo()` for each one. When it's done it calls `stroke()` to draw it to the canvas.

> For all of the methods in Canvas2D that wouldn't normally return a value we will return `this` so we can do function chaining.

The last thing we need to implement is the `onMouseUp()` event handler. All we need to do here is set the `drawing` flag back to `false`:

```
function onMouseUp(e)
{
    penUp();
}
function penUp()
{
    drawing = false;
}
```

What just happened?

We used mouse events to capture and store drawing actions in a buffer. Then we used the canvas API to draw lines to the canvas from those points. Now let's open our application in the browser and check it out. We can scribble on the canvas using the mouse and create simple line drawings.

Changing context properties

Let's take our application to the next level by allowing the user to change the pen properties such as color, opacity, and width.

Time for action – adding context properties

First let's add some code to our `Canvas2D` object to allow us to change the global context drawing properties. Let's set some default values in the constructor. We will set the pen to black with a width of 4 and make it completely opaque by setting `globalAlpha` to 1. We will set the line joins and caps to round to make our lines look smoother:

```
context.lineWidth = 4;
context.strokeStyle = "black";
context.fillStyle = "black";
context.globalAlpha = 1.0;
context.lineJoin = "round";
context.lineCap = "round";
```

Next we'll add public property accessor methods to allow us to set and get the value of the color, opacity, and width properties. If a parameter is passed into a property method (that is, `arguments.length` is not 0) it will set the value of the property then return `this` so we can do function chaining. Otherwise it will return the value of the property:

```
this.penWidth = function(newWidth)
{
    if (arguments.length)
    {
        context.lineWidth = newWidth;
        return this;
    }
    return context.lineWidth;
};
this.penColor = function(newColor)
{
    if (arguments.length)
    {
        context.strokeStyle = newColor;
        context.fillStyle = newColor;
        return this;
    }
    return context.strokeStyle;
};
this.penOpacity = function(newOpacity)
```

```
{
    if (arguments.length)
    {
        context.globalAlpha = newOpacity;
        return this;
    }
    return context
};
```

Now all we need is a way for the user to change these settings from the application, so the next thing we will implement is a toolbar.

Creating a toolbar

Our toolbar will need the following buttons. The first three will be used to change the properties of the context. The last two will allow us to undo and clear the canvas.

- **Color**: This button displays a drop-down menu where the user can choose a pen color
- **Opacity**: This button displays a drop-down menu where the user can choose the pen opacity
- **Width**: This button displays a drop-down menu where the user can choose the pen width
- **Undo**: This button removes the last drawing action
- **Clear**: This button clears the canvas and all drawing actions to start over

Custom data attributes, which we covered in the previous chapter, will be used throughout our toolbar to define actions for the toolbar buttons and options for our menus. We will use these later in our JavaScript to determine the action or option that was selected. Adding a little extra markup now will save us from writing a lot of repetitive code later on.

Time for action – creating a toolbar

You can find the code for this section in `chapter4/example4.2`.

We'll define the toolbar in our HTML file just inside the main element and above the canvas:

```
<div id="toolbar">
  <div class="dropdown-menu">
    <button data-action="menu">Color</button>
    <ul id="color-menu"data-option="penColor" class="menu">
      <li data-value="red"></li>
      <li data-value="orange"></li>
```

```
            <li data-value="yellow"></li>
            <li data-value="green"></li>
            <li data-value="blue"></li>
            <li data-value="purple"></li>
            <li data-value="black" class="selected"></li>
            <li data-value="white"></li>
        </ul>
    </div>
<div class="dropdown-menu">
    <button data-action="menu">Opacity</button>
        <ul data-option="penOpacity" class="menu">
            <li data-value=".1">10%</li>
            <li data-value=".2">20%</li>
            <li data-value=".3">30%</li>
            <li data-value=".4">40%</li>
            <li data-value=".5">50%</li>
            <li data-value=".6">60%</li>
            <li data-value=".7">70%</li>
            <li data-value=".8">80%</li>
            <li data-value=".9">90%</li>
            <li data-value="1" class="selected">100%</li>
        </ul>
    </div>
    <div class="dropdown-menu">
      <button data-action="menu">Width</button>
        <ul id="width-menu" data-option="penWidth" class="menu">
            <li data-value="1">1</li>
            <li data-value="2">2</li>
            <li data-value="4" class="selected">4</li>
            <li data-value="6">6</li>
            <li data-value="8">8</li>
            <li data-value="10">10</li>
            <li data-value="12">12</li>
            <li data-value="14">14</li>
            <li data-value="16">16</li>
        </ul>
    </div> |
    <button data-action="undo">Undo</button> |
    <button data-action="clear">Clear</button>
</div>
```

Each toolbar button has a `data-action` custom attribute. This will be used in JavaScript to determine which action to take when the button is clicked. For the buttons with drop-down menus we set the `data-action` to `"menu"`. The **Undo** and **Clear** buttons each have their own unique action values.

Since the toolbar items for color, opacity, and width are drop-down menus we wrapped them in a `<div class="dropdown-menu">` element. This groups the toolbar button and the menu to display when the button is clicked. The menus are defined using as an unordered list. Each `<ul>` element is given a class of `menu` and a `data-option` custom attribute. The value of this attribute matches to the name of a property method in the `Canvas2D` object, for example `penColor()`.

The menu items are defined with `<li>` elements. Each one has a `data-value` custom attribute. This is set to the value that will be passed into the property method defined by the `data-option` attribute on the menu.

Now let's style the toolbar in CSS:

```
#toolbar
{
    padding: 2px;
    background-color: rgba(0, 0, 0, 0.5);
}
#toolbar button
{
    border: none;
    background-color: transparent;
    color: white;
    font-size: 1em;
}
```

First we make the color of the toolbar black with a 50 percent opacity so the background color bleeds through. Then we style the buttons to remove the borders and background color, and set the text color to white. Now let's style the drop-down menus:

```
#toolbar .dropdown-menu
{
    display: inline-block;
    position: relative;
}
#toolbar ul.menu
{
    display: none;
    position: absolute;
    top: 100%;
    left: 0;
```

```
        margin: 0;
        padding-left: 1.5em;
        border: 1px solid black;
        box-shadow: 2px 2px 8px 1px rgba(0, 0, 0, 0.5);
        background-color: silver;
        color: black;
        list-style-type: none;
    }
```

We set the `<div class="dropdown-menu">`wrapper elements to display `inline-block` and set the `position` to `relative` so that we can absolutely position the menus under them.

For the `<ul>` menu elements first we set `display` to `none` so they are hidden by default. Then we set the `position` to `absolute` so they don't take up any space in the page. To make them appear below the button instead of over it we set `top` to `100%`. Then we give it a shadow to give the illusion of depth. Finally, we get rid of the list bullet points by setting `list-style-type` to `none`.

Finally let's style the menu items:

```
    #toolbar ul.menu>li
    {
        margin: 0;
        min-width: 4em;
        height: 2em;
        border-width: 0;
        background-color: WhiteSmoke;
        font-size: .75em;
        cursor: pointer;
    }
    #toolbar ul.menu>li.selected
    {
        list-style-type: circle;
        background-color: lightblue;
    }
```

We give the menu items a minimum width so they don't get too small. We also specify a style for the selected menu item to display a circle next to it using `list-style-type` and color the background light blue.

What just happened?

We created a toolbar in our HTML file with menu items for color, width, and opacity. We used custom data attributes to define custom actions that will be implemented in our JavaScript. Lastly we styled the menus in our CSS file so they line up under their toolbar buttons.

Time for action – implementing a reusable toolbar

Now let's create a new reusable `Toolbar` object that encapsulates the code for a toolbar. That way we can also use it in our other applications later on. We will put it inside a new file called `toolbar.js`. The constructor will take the root element of the toolbar wrapped in a jQuery object:

```
function Toolbar($toolbar)
{
    var _this = this;
```

Remember how I said in *Chapter 1, The Task at Hand* that the `this` pointer can cause problems when using event handlers with public methods? To get around that we will create a global `_this` variable and set it to the object's `this` so it's always available.

First we will implement the public methods. We have two methods that are used to notify the application that either a toolbar button or menu item has been clicked. In this object they are just placeholders. The client application will override them to implement custom behavior:

```
this.toolbarButtonClicked = function(action)
{
    return false;
};
this.menuItemClicked = function(option, value)
{
    return false;
};
```

The `toolbarButtonClicked()` method takes the button's `data-action` attribute as a parameter. The `menuItemClicked()` method takes the menu's `data-option` and the menu item's `data-value` attribute as parameters.

We also need a public method called `hideMenus()` to hide all of the toolbar's drop-down menus. It just finds all of the menu elements and hides them:

```
this.hideMenus = function()
{
    $(".menu", $toolbar).hide();
}
```

The next thing we will add is an event handler for all of the toolbar buttons:

```
$("button", $toolbar).click(function(e) {
  onToolbarButtonClicked($(this));
});
```

When the user clicks a button in the toolbar, it calls the private onToolbarButtonClicked() method passing it the button that was clicked wrapped in a jQuery object. Let's implement that handler now:

```
function onToolbarButtonClicked($button)
{
    var action = $button.data("action");
    if (!_this.toolbarButtonClicked(action))
    {
        if (action == "menu")
        {
            showMenu($button.siblings("ul.menu"));
        }
        else
        {
            _this.hideMenus();
        }
    }
}
```

This method gets the value of the data-action custom attribute from the button. Then it passes it into the public toolbarButtonClicked() method. Notice that it must use _this to call the public methods because this is currently pointing at the window object. If toolbarButtonClicked() returns true it means that the client handled the action and there's nothing else to do. Otherwise it checks if the action was "menu" and if so, calls showMenu() passing in the menu element, which is a sibling of the button. If it's not, the menu action it hides all the menus.

Now let's write the private showMenu() method:

```
function showMenu($menu)
{
    if ($menu.is(":visible"))
    {
        $menu.fadeOut("fast");
    }
    else
    {
        // Hide any open menus
        _this.hideMenus();
```

```
        // Show this menu
        $menu.fadeIn("fast");
    }
}
```

We use the jQuery `is()` method passing in the `:visible` filter to determine if the menu is already showing. If it is, it fades the menu out to hide it. Otherwise it hides all of the menus in the toolbar, in case another one is open, and then fades the menu in to show it.

Next we add the click event handler for all of the menu items:

```
$(".menu>li", $toolbar).click(function(e) {
    onMenuItemClicked($(this));
});
```

When the user clicks a menu item in the toolbar it calls `onMenuItemClicked()` passing it the menu item that was clicked wrapped in a jQuery object:

```
function onMenuItemClicked($item)
{
    var $menu = $item.parent();
    var option = $menu.data("option");
    var value = $item.data("value");
    if (!_this.menuItemClicked(option, value))
    {
        $item.addClass("selected")
            .siblings().removeClass("selected");
        $menu.fadeOut("fast");
    }
}
```

First we get the parent element which is the menu. Then we get the `data-option` attribute from it. Next we get the `data-value` attribute from the menu item itself. We pass those values as parameters to the public `menuItemClicked()` method. If that method returns `true` it means that the client handled the action and there's nothing else to do. Otherwise we add a `"selected"` class to the menu item to highlight it and remove the class from all of the other menu items. Then we fade the menu out to hide it.

What just happened?

We created a reusable object that encapsulates toolbar behavior including buttons and dropdown menus. It uses custom data attributes to define the actions for toolbar buttons and menu items. We can use this object in our applications whenever we need a toolbar.

Adding a toolbar

Now that we have a `Toolbar` object and the HTML for our toolbar and menus defined we can hook up events in our drawing application to handle user interaction.

Time for action – adding the toolbar object

Let's add the `Toolbar` object to our application. First we add a `toolbar` variable to `CanvasPadApp` and set it to a new instance of the `Toolbar` object. We pass in the toolbar's root `<div>` element as a parameter to the constructor:

```
var version = "4.2",
canvas2d = new Canvas2D($("#main>canvas")),
toolbar = new Toolbar($("#toolbar")),
        // code not shown...
```

In `start()` we override the `toolbar` object's `toolbarButtonClicked()` and `menuItemClicked()` methods to set them to our own implementations to handle those events:

```
toolbar.toolbarButtonClicked = toolbarButtonClicked;
toolbar.menuItemClicked = menuItemClicked;
```

First let's implement our `CanvasPadApp.toolbarButtonClicked()` method:

```
function toolbarButtonClicked(action)
{
    switch (action)
    {
        case "clear":
            if (confirm("Clear the canvas?"))
            {
                actions = [];
                redraw();
            }
            break;
        case "undo":
            actions.pop();
            redraw();
            break;
    }
}
```

When the user clicks the **Clear** button we confirm that they want to clear the canvas. If so we set the `actions` array to a new array to clear everything out and then call `redraw()`, which clears the canvas.

When the user clicks the **Undo** button it removes the last drawing action from the `actions` array, then calls `redraw()`.

Now let's implement the `menuItemClicked()` method. It takes two parameters; the menu option name and the value of the menu item that was selected:

```
function menuItemClicked(option, value)
{
    canvas2d[option](value);
}
```

If you remember from earlier instances, the `data-option` attribute is the name of the method that is used to set the property in the `Canvas2D` object. We use the square brace method of accessing that method in the object, and then we execute it passing the `data-value` attribute from the menu item into it.

For example, if the user clicked the red menu item in the **Color** menu, the `data-option` would be `"penColor"` and the `data-value` would be `"red"`. So in this case the statement `canvas2d[option](value)` would be equivalent to calling `canvas2d.penColor("red")`.

What just happened?

We added the reusable `Toolbar` object we created in the previous section to our application and added event handlers to handle toolbar button and menu events. Then we implemented the undo and clear actions.

Time for action – initializing menu items

Next we will initialize the **Color** menu to set the background color of each item to the color it represents. We could do that in CSS but it would be cumbersome. Instead we are going to write a JavaScript method to set them all with just a little bit of code:

```
function initColorMenu()
{
    $("#color-menu li").each(function(i, e) {
        $(e).css("background-color", $(e).data("value"));
    });
}
```

This gets all of the color menu items and iterates over them using the jQuery `each()` method. For each item it sets the background color using the jQuery `css()` method to the value of the `data-value` custom attribute, which is a CSS color name. Just like that we have a menu of colors.

We want to do something similar for the width menu's items, except we will set the bottom border to the width in the `data-value` custom attribute to give the user some idea of how big the line will be:

```
function initWidthMenu()
{
    $("#width-menu li").each(function(i, e) {
        $(e).css("border-bottom",
                 $(e).data("value") + "px solid black");
    });
}
```

We will call these two methods from the `start()` method when we're initializing the application.

What just happened?

We changed the styles for the color and width menu items to give them colors and widths respectively so that the user can better see what they are selecting from the menus.

Now if you open the application in the browser you can change the pen's properties. Go ahead and draw a few lines. If you click on **Undo,** the last line is erased. When you click on **Clear**, the entire drawing is erased.

Adding drawing actions

You may have noticed that when you changed an option, the next time you drew something the options applied to all of the previous lines that were drawn. That's not a very good user experience. The user expects that when they change the pen options it will only apply to the next thing they draw, not everything.

In order to get that to work properly we will need to add more data to each action than just a list of points. We also need to know the color, width, and opacity to draw the points with. For that we need an object to hold all of these values.

Time for action – creating drawing actions

We will use a factory method to create this object. Let's add a newAction() method to CanvasPadApp that creates the action object for us with the current drawing options set:

```
function newAction(tool)
{
    return {
        tool: tool,
        color: canvas2d.penColor(),
        width: canvas2d.penWidth(),
        opacity: canvas2d.penOpacity(),
        points: []
    };
}
```

The newAction() method takes one parameter which is the name of the drawing tool the action will use. Next it uses curly braces to define a new object literal. The object will hold the tool, the context property values, and the points for that action. It gets the current color, width, and opacity settings from our Canvas2D object.

The next thing we need to do is remove the global points variable from the CanvasPadApp object and replace it with a curAction variable to hold the current action object created by newAction(). Let's also add a curTool variable to hold the current tool, and set it to "pen":

```
varversion = "4.2",
    // code not shown...
  curTool = "pen",
  curAction = newAction(curTool),
    actions = [];
```

Now, wherever we used the points variable before we will need to change it to use curAction.points instead. The first spot is the penDown() method:

```
function penDown(pageX, pageY)
{
    drawing = true;
    curAction = newAction(curTool);
    curAction.points.push(
        canvas2d.getCanvasPoint(pageX, pageY));
    actions.push(curAction);
}
```

First we set curAction to a new action object, and then add the first point to the curAction object's points array. Then we add curAction to the actions array.

The next stop is the `penMoved()` method. There we add the next point to the action's `points` array:

```
function penMoved(pageX, pageY)
{
    var canvasPoint = canvas2d.getCanvasPoint(pageX, pageY);
    showCoordinates(canvasPoint);
    if (drawing)
    {
        curAction.points.push(canvasPoint);
        redraw();
    }
}
```

We also need to update the `penUp()` method:

```
function penUp()
{
    if (drawing)
    {
        drawing = false;
        if (curAction.points.length < 2)
        {
            actions.pop();
        }
    }
}
```

First we check the `drawing` variable to make sure we are indeed drawing. If so we turn off the `drawing` flag by setting it to `false`. Next we need to make sure there are at least two points in the action's `points` array. If the user pressed the mouse button but didn't move it, there would only be one point. We can't draw anything without two points so we'll just remove that action from the `actions` array using `pop()`.

Lastly, we will update the `redraw()` method. Here's where we need to make some substantial changes:

```
function redraw()
{
    canvas2d.clear();
    canvas2d.savePen();

    for (var i in actions)
    {
        var action = actions[i];
        canvas2d.penColor(action.color)
                .penWidth(action.width)
```

```
                    .penOpacity(action.opacity);

            canvas2d.drawPoints(action.points);
        }

        canvas2d.restorePen();
    }
```

First of all notice the calls to `savePen()` and `restorePen()` in the `Canvas2D` object. They will save the current context properties before we start drawing all of the actions and then restore them when we are done. We will implement those in a moment. Next we iterate over all of the actions setting the pen color, width, and opacity for each one (using function chaining) before drawing the points.

What just happened?

We added a drawing action object to keep track of the tool, pen properties, and points for each drawing action. Now when we change drawing properties they don't affect previous actions.

Time for action – saving and restoring

Now, about those `savePen()` and `restorePen()` methods. Let's go on over to `canvas2d.js` and add them to the `Canvas2D` object. We could keep track of the current properties ourselves, but the canvas API provides an easier way.

The canvas API contains both `save()` and `restore()` methods. Any time you need to save the state of the context you call `save()` and it pushes the state of the context on to a stack. When you want to restore the context state you call `restore()` and it pops the state off the stack back into the context. This allows you to save and restore the state multiple times recursively.

This works great for situations where you may have a library of drawing functions that could be drawn in any order at runtime. Each method can call `save()` before it starts changing context properties and call `restore()` when it's done. That way when a method is done the context is in the same state that it was before the method was called:

```
this.savePen = function()
{
    context.save();
    return this;
};
this.restorePen = function()
{
    context.restore();
    return this;
};
```

What just happened?

We learned how to save the context and restore it so that we don't lose the context's current properties.

Let's open the application in the browser and take a look. Now we can draw in all different colors, widths, and opacities. If you make a mistake you can click on **Undo** to erase it. And if you want to start all over you can click on **Clear**.

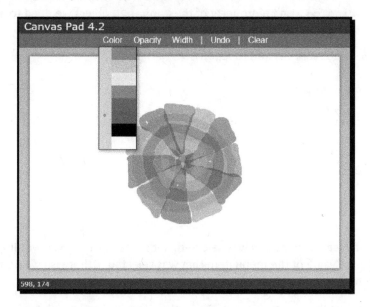

Adding drawing tools

At this point we have an application where we can draw simple lines such as a pen, but it sure would be nice if we could draw some shapes such as straight lines, rectangles, and circles. In this section we will add a **Tool** menu to allow the user to select different shapes to draw.

Time for action – adding a line tool

You can find the code for this section in chapter4/example4.3.

Currently we can draw freehand lines, but we don't have a way to draw a straight line from one point to another. So let's add a line drawing tool. To allow the user to select different tools we need a new drop-down menu toolbar option. Let's add it to our HTML:

```
<div id="toolbar">
  <div class="dropdown-menu">
    <button data-action="menu">Tool</button>
```

```
       <uldata-option="drawingTool" class="menu">
         <li data-value="pen" class="selected">Pen</li>
         <li data-value="line">Line</li>
       </ul>
     </div>
```

For this menu we are setting the `data-option` attribute to `drawingTool`. We add menu items for the **Pen** tool, which we currently have, and a **Line** tool, which we are implementing now. Since `drawingTool` isn't a property of the `Canvas2D` object we need to add code to check for it in `menuItemClicked()`:

```
function menuItemClicked(option, value)
{
    switch (option)
    {
        case "drawingTool":
            curTool = value;
            break;
        default;
            canvas2d[option](value);
    }
}
```

First we check to see which option was selected. If it's `"drawingTool"` we simply set the current tool to the value of the menu item that was selected. Otherwise we do the default behavior of setting the `Canvas2D` property with the selected value.

Next we will change the `penMoved()` method. We need to check which tool we are currently using. If it's the pen we add another point to the `points` array. Otherwise we only want to change the second point in the `points` array because we are drawing a straight line, and a line only has two points:

```
function penMoved(pageX, pageY)
{
    var canvasPoint = canvas2d.getCanvasPoint(pageX, pageY);
    showCoordinates(canvasPoint);

    if (drawing)
    {
        if (curTool == "pen")
        {
            // Add another point
            curAction.points.push(canvasPoint);
        }
        else
```

```
        {
            // Change the second point
            curAction.points[1] = canvasPoint;
        }
        redraw();
    }
}
```

Lastly we need to make some changes to the `redraw()` method. Inside the loop we will check the action's tool. If it's the pen we call `canvas2d.drawPoints()` the same as we did before. If it's the line tool we call `canvas2d.drawLine()` passing in the two points:

```
function redraw()
{
    canvas2d.clear();
    canvas2d.savePen();

    for (var i in actions)
    {
        var action = actions[i];
        canvas2d.penColor(action.color)
                .penWidth(action.width)
                .penOpacity(action.opacity);

        switch (action.tool)
        {
            case "pen":
                canvas2d.drawPoints(action.points);
                break;
            case "line":
                canvas2d.drawLine(action.points[0],
                    action.points[1]);
                break;
        }
    }
    canvas2d.restorePen();
}
```

Wait a minute! We don't have a `drawLine()` method in the `Canvas2D` object yet. So let's go add it:

```
this.drawLine = function(point1, point2)
{
    context.beginPath();
    context.moveTo(point1.x, point1.y);
```

```
        context.lineTo(point2.x, point2.y);
            context.stroke();
            return this;
    };
```

The drawLine() method takes the line start and end points as parameters. After beginning a new path it moves to the first point, draws a line to the second point, and then strokes it. That's it. Now we can draw straight lines.

What just happened?

We added a **Tool** menu to our toolbar where the user can select different drawing tools. In addition to the pen tool we already had, we added a line drawing tool to draw straight lines in our application.

Drawing rectangles

You could draw a rectangle using paths, but the canvas API has a couple built in methods to do this; drawRect() and fillRect(). They both take the same parameters; *x*, *y*, width, and height. drawRect() uses the strokeStyle to draw the lines and fillRect() uses the fillStyle to fill it.

The following draws a rectangle starting at the point (350, 10) with a width of 50 and a height of 90:

```
        context.strokeRect(350, 10, 50, 90);
```

This example draws a filled rectangle starting at the point (425, 10) with a width of 50 and a height of 90:

```
        context.fillRect(425, 10, 50, 90);
```

Time for action – adding a rectangle tool

Let's add a tool to draw rectangles. We'll start by adding a menu item to the **Tool** drop-down menu with its data-value attribute set to "rect":

```
    <li data-value="rect">Rectangle</li>
```

Let's implement the `drawRect()` method in `Canvas2D`:

```
this.drawRect = function(point1, point2, fill)
{
    var w = point2.x - point1.x,
        h = point2.y - point1.y;
    if (fill) context.fillRect(point1.x, point1.y, w, h);
    else context.strokeRect(point1.x, point1.y, w, h);
    return this;
};
```

Our `drawRect()` method takes three parameters; the two points that define top-left and bottom-right coordinates, and a Boolean value to determine if the rectangle should be filled. Since `fillRect()` and `strokeRect()` both take width and height parameters we need to compute them by subtracting the `point1` variable's coordinates from `point2` variable's coordinates.

Before we code up the call to `drawRect()` there is one piece of business we need to take care of. Our `drawRect()` method can draw either outlined or filled rectangles, so we need a way to let the user pick which one they want. Let's add another drop-down menu to the toolbar named **Fill** that allows the user to set this option:

```
<div class="dropdown-menu">
  <button data-action="menu">Fill</button>
    <ul data-option="fillShapes" class="menu">
      <li data-value="true" class="selected">Yes</li>
      <li data-value="false">No</li>
    </ul>
</div>
```

The drop-down menu has only two options: **Yes** and **No**. In our `CanvasPadApp` object we need a global `fillShapes` Boolean variable to keep track of the current setting. Let's add this at the top of the object along with our other variables:

```
var version = "4.3",
    // code not shown...
  fillShapes = true;
```

We also need to add it to the action object in the `newAction()` method. We will add a field named `fill` and set it to the current value of `fillShapes`:

```
function newAction(tool)
{
    return {
        tool: tool,
        color: canvas2d.penColor(),
```

```
        width: canvas2d.penWidth(),
        opacity: canvas2d.penOpacity(),
        fill: fillShapes,
        points: []
    };
}
```

Next we need to add some extra code to the `menuItemClicked()` method to check if the option was the **Fill** menu option and if so set the `fillShapes` variable to its `data-value`. Since the value is either `"true"` or `"false"` we can convert it directly to a Boolean:

```
function menuItemClicked(option, value)
{
    switch (option)
    {
        case "drawingTool":
            curTool = value;
            break;
        case "fillShapes":
            fillShapes = Boolean(value);
            break;
        default:
            canvas2d[option](value);
    }
}
```

Okay, that's it for the **Fill** option. Now we can add the code to the `redraw()` method to check for the rectangle tool and draw it by calling `drawRect()`. We will pass in the two points of the rectangle and the value of `action.fill` to tell it whether to fill the rectangle or not:

```
switch (action.tool)
{
    // code not shown...
    case "rect":
        canvas2d.drawRect(action.points[0],
            action.points[1],
            action.fill);
        break;
}
```

What just happened?

We added a rectangle tool to our **Tool** menu. We also added a new toolbar menu to select whether to fill shapes or not. We used this to determine whether to draw filled or outlined rectangles.

Arcs and circles

In addition to straight lines you can draw arcs, or portions of a circle, using the context's `arc()` method. It takes the following parameters:

```
arc(centerX, centerY, radius, startAngle, endAngle, clockwise)
```

- ◆ `centerX`: This parameter tells the horizontal position of the center point.
- ◆ `centerY`: This parameter tells the vertical position of the center point.
- ◆ `radius`: This parameter tells the radius of the arc.
- ◆ `startAngle`: This parameter tells the starting angle of the arc specified in radians. It can be any value between 0 to 2π. Numbers outside this range will automatically be normalized into it.
- ◆ `endAngle`: This parameter tells the ending angle of the arc specified in radians. It can be any value between 0 to 2π.
- ◆ `counterclockwise`: This is a `Boolean` parameter that specifies which direction to draw the arc from start to end angle. If false it draws clockwise, if true counterclockwise.

Arcs are really paths, so you must use `beginPath()` and `stroke()` to draw them. The following code draws the bottom-right corner of a circle. The center is at the point `(100, 200)`. It has a radius of `40`. The angle starts at `0` and ends at $\pi/2$ radians, or 90 degrees. And it is drawn clockwise:

```
context.beginPath();
context.arc(100, 200, 40, 0, Math.PI / 2, false);
context.stroke();
```

You can draw a full circle using the `arc()` method too. A circle is simply a complete arc drawn from 0 to 2π radians, or 360 degrees:

```
context.beginPath();
context.arc(100, 200, 40, 0, 2 * Math.PI, false);
context.stroke();
```

If you are unfamiliar with radians, let me give you a brief overview. Radians are simply another way to specify an angle. It is based on the formula for the circumference of a circle; C = 2 * π * radius. By setting the radius to 1, we can use that formula to measure the length of an arc from one point on the circle to another point along the circumference. If you were to measure all the way around a circle you would have 2π radians. Therefore, 2π radians are equal to 360 degrees. Half way around the circle is π radians, which is equal to 180 degrees. One quarter of the way around is π/2 radians or 90 degrees.

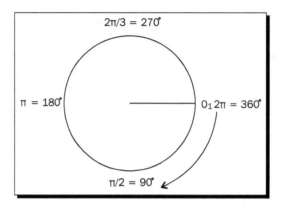

If you prefer to use degrees you can always use this conversion function to convert degrees to radians:

```
function toRadians(deg)
{
    return deg * Math.PI / 180;
}
```

Here are some examples of arcs using different parameters. Arcs 1 and 2 use the same start and end angles, just drawing in different direction. The same is true for arcs 3 and 4. Arc 5 draws a complete circle:

- `context.arc(100, 200, 40, 0, toRadians(90), true);`
- `context.arc(200, 200, 40, 0, toRadians(90), false);`
- `context.arc(300, 200, 40, 0, toRadians(180), true);`
- `context.arc(400, 200, 40, 0, toRadians(180), false);`
- `context.arc(500, 200, 40, 0, toRadians(360), false);`

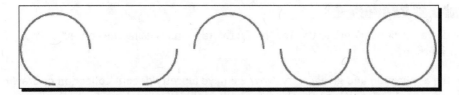

Time for action – adding a circle tool

Let's add a circle menu item to our **Tool** menu:

```
<li data-value="circle">Circle</li>
```

Now let's go ahead and add a drawCircle() method to Canvas2D. Our method will take the center point, the radius, and a Boolean value to determine if the circle should be filled:

```
this.drawCircle = function(center, radius, fill)
{
    context.beginPath();
    context.arc(center.x, center.y, radius, 0, 2 * Math.PI, true)
    if (fill) context.fill();
    else context.stroke();
    return this;
};
```

If the fill parameter is set to true we call context.fill() after calling arc().
Otherwise we just use context.stroke() to draw the outline.

Finally let's add the code to redraw() to draw the circle. Here we need to do a little work to find the radius to pass into drawCircle(). First we find the difference in x between the first and second point, then the difference in y. Whichever one is smaller we will use that as our radius:

```
switch (action.tool)
{
    // code not shown...
    case "circle":
        var dx = Math.abs(action.points[1].x -
            action.points[0].x);
        var dy = Math.abs(action.points[1].y -
            action.points[0].y);
        var radius = Math.min(dx, dy);
        canvas2d.drawRect(action.points[0], radius,
            action.fill);
        break;
}
```

What just happened?

We added a new menu item to the **Tool** menu to draw circles using the context's `arc()` method.

Open the application and give it a try. Now we have a pretty decent collection of drawing tools in our application. We can make some more sophisticated drawings with all different colors and opacities rather than just black scribbles.

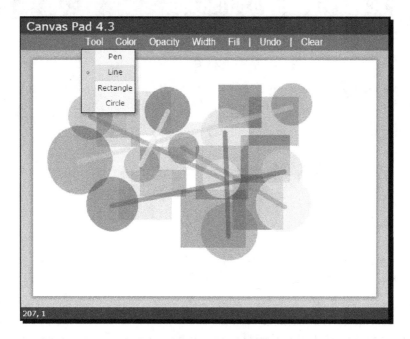

Have a go hero

Try adding your own drawing tool, such as a triangle or some other shape. Implement the drawing of the shape in the `Canvas2D` object then add a menu item to the toolbar.

Pop quiz

Q1. What unit is used to define the angle when drawing arcs?

1. Degrees
2. Units
3. Radians
4. Arcs

Q2. What context method is used to draw a path to the canvas?

1. `drawPath()`

2. `stroke()`

3. `draw()`

4. `endPath()`

Summary

In this chapter, we created a drawing application called canvas pad which can be used to make simple drawings. Along the way we learned how to use the HTML5 canvas element and API. We also learned how to implement a reusable toolbar with menu items that are bound to actions using custom data attributes. We now have a reusable toolbar we can use in other applications.

We covered the following concepts in this chapter:

◆ How to use the `<canvas>` element and the canvas API

◆ How to get a canvas context and change global drawing properties such as width, color, and opacity

◆ How to use paths to draw free lines and shapes

◆ How to draw lines, rectangles, and circles

◆ How to get the position of the mouse inside a canvas element

◆ How to create a reusable toolbar and implement drop-down menus

◆ How to use custom data attributes to bind actions to menu items

In the next chapter we will continue our exploration of the canvas. We will learn some more advanced canvas features such as transformations and rotations. We will also see how to load images and export them from the canvas, in the process touching upon the file API. Then we will get down to the individual pixels of the canvas to do some image manipulation.

5
Not So Blank Canvas

"This world is but a canvas to our imagination."

– Henry David Thoreau

In the previous chapter we learned the basics of using the HTML5 canvas. We created a drawing application called Canvas Pad with tools to draw lines and shapes in all different colors and sizes. In this chapter we will continue our exploration of the Canvas API by extending Canvas Pad to add more tools. Then we will create a new application called Photo Pad where we will take a look at how to load images using the File API and perform image processing by accessing and modifying the individual pixels of the canvas.

In this chapter we will learn:

- How to get text input and draw it to the canvas
- How to use the Canvas API transformation functions to change how items are drawn on the canvas
- How to export the canvas image to save it
- How to load images using the HTML5 File API
- How to draw bitmap images to the canvas
- How to get the data for each pixel in a canvas, manipulate it, and put it back

Drawing text

There are two methods available to draw text on the canvas: `strokeText()` and `fillText()`. `strokeText()` draws outlined text using the current `lineWidth` and `strokeStyle`, while `fillText()` draws with the current `fillStyle`. Both take the same parameters; the text to draw, and the x and y coordinates. The context object has a global font property to define which `font` to use. You set its value the same you would when defining a font in CSS. Continuing where we left off in the previous chapter with our Canvas Pad application, we will add a new text drawing tool. You can find the source code for this section in `Chapter 5/example5.1`.

Time for action – adding a text tool

Let's start by adding a new item to the Tool drop-down menu for the text tool:

```
<li data-value="text">Text</li>
```

Next, we'll add a `drawText()` method to the `Canvas2D` object. It will take the text to draw, a point from where to draw the text, and a Boolean value indicating whether to fill the text or just outline it. If `fill` is `true`, it uses `fillText()` to draw the text, otherwise it uses `strokeText()`:

```
this.drawText = function(text, point, fill)
{
    if (fill)
    {
        context.fillText(text, point.x, point.y);
    }
    else
    {
        context.strokeText(text, point.x, point.y);
    }
};
```

Now we need a way to allow the user to enter the text that he/she wants to draw. We will need a text input field that we will keep hidden until the user wants to add some text. When the user selects the text tool and clicks on the canvas, we will position the text field where he/she clicked on and wait for him/her to enter the text. When the user presses the *Enter* key, we will hide the text field and draw the text to the canvas.

To make it seem like the user is typing on the canvas, we need to set a couple more properties in the canvas context for the font. We will set the `font` and `textBaseline` properties in the constructor. The baseline tells the context where to draw the text relative to the position. We will set it to `"top"` so it will draw the top of the text at the y position, which is the same place our text field will be. Other common baseline values are `"bottom"` and `"middle"`:

```
context.font = "24px Verdana, Geneva, sans-serif";
context.textBaseline = "top";
```

Now we need a text field for the user to enter text. Let's add it to the bottom of our HTML file, after the footer element:

```
<div id="text-input">
    <input type="text" />
</div>
```

Next let's go into our CSS and define the style for the text-input element. We will set display to none, so that it is hidden, and set position to absolute, so that we can position it wherever we want to on the page. We will also change the size of the font to 24 pixels because that's what we set for our font size in the context:

```
#text-input
{
    display: none;
    position: absolute;
    width: 8em;
}
#text-input>input
{
    font-size: 24px;
}
```

Now let's add some JavaScript code to the penDown() method in CanvasPadApp so that when the user clicks the mouse it shows the text input field:

```
function penDown(pageX, pageY)
{
    if (curTool == "text")
    {
        // Check if it's already visible
        if ($("#text-input").is(":visible")) return;
        showTextInput(pageX, pageY);
    }
    else
    {
        drawing = true;
    }

    // code not shown...
}
```

First it checks the current tool. If it is the text tool, it checks to see if the text field is already visible and if so, there's no need to continue. Otherwise it calls showTextInput() passing in the mouse coordinates. Notice that we don't set drawing to true in this case because we don't need to track the mouse.

The showTextInput() method takes the mouse coordinates and moves the text-input element to the point where the user clicked the mouse on the canvas:

```
function showTextInput(pageX, pageY)
{
    $("#text-input").css("top", pageY)
                    .css("left", pageX)
                    .fadeIn("fast");
    $("#text-input input").val("").focus();
}
```

First we set the top and left CSS properties to move the element over to where the user clicked on and then fade it in. Then it resets the value of the text field and sets the focus on it so the user can start typing. This will make it appear that the user is typing on the canvas.

When the user is done typing, he/she can press the *Enter* key to finish the text. We need to add a keydown event handler to the text field to check for this. We will add that in the start() method:

```
$("#text-input input").keydown(function(e) {
    checkTextInput(e.which);
});
```

The handler calls checkTextInput(), passing in the key code of the key that was pressed. The key code is found in the which field of the event object:

```
function checkTextInput(key)
{
    if (key == 13) // Enter key
    {
        curAction.text = $("#text-input input").val();
        $("#text-input").hide();
        redraw();
    }
    else if (key == 27) // Escape
    {
        actions.pop();
        $("#text-input").hide();
    }
}
```

The checkTextInput() method looks at the key code to see what to do. If the user pressed the *Enter* key, which is key code 13, it will set the text into the current action object, hide the text input, and then call redraw(). If the key code is 27, which is the *Escape* key, it will cancel the text by removing the action and then hiding the text input.

The final piece to implement is the change to `redraw()`. We need to add the text action to our `switch` statement. It passes in the text, the position to draw it, and whether to fill it or not:

```
switch (action.tool)
{
    // code not shown...
    case "text":
        canvas2d.drawText(action.text, action.points[0],
            action.fill);
        break;
}
```

What just happened?

We added a Text tool to our application that allows the user to type text on the canvas and draw it filled or outlined.

Have a go hero

Try adding a toolbar menu for the user to select different font sizes. You will need to change the font size in the canvas context as well as the text input field's style.

Transformations

The Canvas API contains four methods for transforming how things are drawn on the canvas. They change the coordinate system of the canvas so that when you draw something, it draws at a different place than it normally would. Think of it as taking a piece of paper and moving it or rotating it before drawing on it.

- `translate(x, y)`: This translates anything drawn on the canvas by the values specified. The values can be any decimal number. Negative numbers translate up and to the left. Often you will use `translate()` to translate to the center of a shape before applying other transformations to it.

- `scale(x, y)`: This scales anything drawn to the canvas by the values specified. The parameters can be any positive decimal number. If you wanted everything to be drawn half size, you would use scale (0.5, 0.5). If you wanted to double the size, scale (2, 2).

- `rotate(angle)`: This rotates the canvas by an angle. The angle is specified in radians from 0 to 2π. Negative numbers will rotate counterclockwise.

- `transform(a, b, c, d, e, f)`: If none of the other transformation methods work for you, you can use `transform()` to create your own. I wouldn't recommend it unless you know how to use transformation matrices.

Time for action – adding an Ellipse tool

Let's use some transformations to draw an ellipse in Canvas Pad. An ellipse is basically a squashed circle. We can use the `scale()` method to change the scale of either the x or y axis before drawing a circle to squash it into an ellipse. Let's add a `drawEllipse()` method to the `Canvas2D` object. It takes a center point, an end point, and a Boolean to determine if it should be filled:

```
this.drawEllipse = function(center, endPoint, fill)
{
    var rx = Math.abs(endPoint.x - center.x);
    var ry = Math.abs(endPoint.y - center.y);
    var radius = Math.max(rx, ry);
    var scaleX = rx / radius;
    var scaleY = ry / radius;

    context.save();
    context.translate(center.x, center.y);
    context.scale(scaleX, scaleY);
    context.beginPath();
    context.arc(0, 0, radius, 0, Math.PI * 2, true);
    context.closePath();
    if (fill) context.fill();
    else context.stroke();
    context.restore();

    return this;
};
```

There's a lot going on in here, so let's break it down:

1. First we find the horizontal and vertical radii (rx and ry) by calculating the distance between the end point and the center point coordinates. Whichever one is the largest will be the radius of the ellipse.

2. Next we find the horizontal and vertical scales by dividing the radii by the max radius. Since one of the radii is the max radius, that scale will be 1. The other will be scaled less than 1.

3. Next we call `save()` to save the state of the context before we start transforming it.

4. Now we do our transformations. First we translate to the center of the ellipse, so it will transform around the center of the shape. Then we scale by the amounts we calculated previously.

5. Then we draw the circle with `beginPath()`, `arc()`, and `closePath()`. Since the canvas is scaled on one axis, the circle will be squashed into an ellipse.

6. Then we call either `fill()` or `stroke()` depending on the `fill` parameter to draw the circle to the canvas.

7. Finally we call `restore()` to restore the context to the way it was before we applied the transformations, and we're done.

Now that we have a method to draw an ellipse, we can go add an Ellipse menu item to the Tool menu in our HTML:

```
<li data-value="ellipse">Ellipse</li>
```

The only thing left to do is add an option for the Ellipse tool in the `switch` statement in `redraw()` and we're done:

```
switch (action.tool)
{
    // code not shown...
    case "ellipse":
        canvas2d.drawEllipse(action.points[0], action.points[1],
            action.fill);
        break;
}
```

What just happened?

We added an Ellipse tool to our application and implemented a method to draw an ellipse on the canvas using transformations to squash a circle on one axis.

Time for action – exporting an image

We can draw pictures with our Canvas Pad application, but what's the point if we can't save them? HTML5 doesn't have the capability to save files directly to the user's file system because of the security risks. So our options on the client side are pretty limited. We can save the data to `localStorage` or we can open the image in a new browser window, where the user can save the image using the browser's **Save** option. We will do the latter because it allows the user to get a real image file they can use.

You can get the image data as a URL from a canvas by calling the `toDataURL()` method on the canvas element itself (not the context). Then you can open the image URL in another window using `window.open()`. Let's add a **Save** button to our toolbar and set the `data-action` attribute to `"save"`:

```
<button data-action="save">Save</button>
```

Next let's add a check for the action in the `switch` statement of the `toolbarButtonClicked()` method. When the **Save** button is clicked, it will get the data URL and then open it:

```
switch (action.tool)
{
    // code not shown...
    case "save":
        var url = $("#main>canvas")[0].toDataURL();
        window.open(url, "CanvasPadImage");
        break;
}
```

What just happened?

Now we can export images from the canvas using the context's `toDataUrl()` method and open them in another browser window so they can be saved by the user.

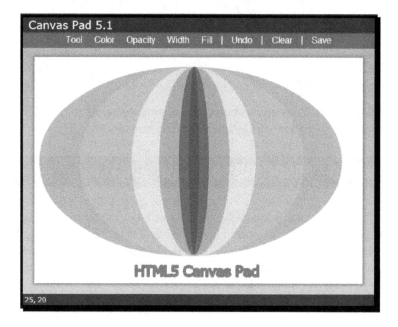

Handling touch events

One of the great things about HTML5 is that you can write one application and it will work on many different devices. Canvas Pad works great as a desktop application where mouse events are available. But it would work just as well on a touch screen device. So let's add support for touch events to the application.

Touch events are similar to mouse events. One difference is that the user can touch the screen with more than one finger, so touch events may contain multiple points. So we will have to take that into consideration when handling them.

There are three basic touch events that browsers support.

- ◆ `touchstart`: We get this event when the user touches the screen. This is equivalent to the `mousedown` event.

- ◆ `touchmove`: We get these events after `touchstart` when the user moves his/her finger on the screen. This is equivalent to the `mousemove` event.

- ◆ `touchend`: We get this event when the user lifts his/her finger off the screen. This is equivalent to the `mouseup` event.

The touch event object that is passed to the event handler contains an array called `touches`. This array contains all of the points that were touched. Each object in the `touches` array has a `pageX` and a `pageY` field, just like mouse events.

You can test whether touch events are supported by checking if the document element has an `ontouchstart` method:

```
var touchSupported = "ontouchstart" in document.documentElement;
```

jQuery doesn't include support for touch events, but it would be nice if we could use the same jQuery mechanism to add touch event handlers to elements. So let's write a jQuery extension to add it. We will create a new file called `touchEvents.js` to put our extension in, so that we can reuse it in other applications.

Time for action – adding touch event handlers

Extending the jQuery library is actually pretty easy. First we wrap our extensions in an immediately invoked function expression and pass the jQuery object into it. This is a best practice to make sure the dollar sign is really mapped to jQuery and not being used by something else. Then we define our extension methods by adding them to jQuery's internal `$.fn` object:

```
(function($)
{
    $.fn.touchstart = function(handler)
    {
        this.each(function(i, e) {
            e.addEventListener("touchstart", handler); });
        return this;
    };
    $.fn.touchmove = function(handler)
```

```
        {
            this.each(function(i, e) {
                e.addEventListener("touchmove", handler); });
            return this;
        };

        $.fn.touchend = function(handler)
        {
            this.each(function(i, e) {
                e.addEventListener("touchend", handler); });
            return this;
        };

        $.isTouchSupported =
            ("ontouchstart" in document.documentElement);
    })(jQuery);
```

 Note that in an extension method's context, the `this` pointer refers to the jQuery object that wraps the selected elements. So `this.each()` iterates over each of the elements that were selected.

The `touchstart`, `touchmove`, and `touchend` methods all work the same way. They iterate over the elements and call `addEventListener()` for each one.

We also defined a global `isTouchSupported` variable directly on the jQuery object. It checks for touch support using the method described previously. We will use that to determine if we should use touch or mouse events in our application.

 You can learn more about writing jQuery extensions on the jQuery website (`http://jquery.com`).

Our extension is done, so let's go back to `CanvasPadApp` and add the code to our application to handle touch events. First in the `start()` method we need to check if touch is supported and wire up the correct events:

```
    if ($.isTouchSupported)
    {
        $("#main>canvas").touchstart(onTouchStart)
            .touchmove(onTouchMove)
            .touchend(onTouchEnd);
    }
    else
    {
```

```
$("#main>canvas").mousedown(onMouseDown)
    .mousemove(onMouseMove)
    .mouseup(onMouseUp)
    .mouseout(onMouseUp);
}
```

The `onTouchStart()` event handler method must call both `stopPropagation()` and `preventDefault()` on the event object to keep it from performing the default behavior. Otherwise it might try to drag the screen rather than draw on the canvas:

```
function onTouchStart(e)
{
    e.stopPropagation();
    e.preventDefault();
    penDown(e.touches[0].pageX, e.touches[0].pageY);
}
```

Next we extract the point that the user touched. There could be multiple points, but we are only interested in the first point in the `touches` array. We extract the `pageX` and `pageY` fields from it and pass them into the `penDown()` method.

The `onTouchMove()` handler works the same way except it calls `penMoved()`:

```
function onTouchMove(e)
{
    e.stopPropagation();
    e.preventDefault();
    penMoved(e.touches[0].pageX, e.touches[0].pageY);
}
```

The `onTouchEnd()` handler simply calls `penUp()`, the same as `onMouseUp()`:

```
function onTouchEnd(e)
{
    penUp();
}
```

What just happened?

We created a reusable jQuery extension to add touch events to any element and added touch support to our application. We now have a drawing application that can be used to draw on both desktop and mobile devices.

With that our Canvas Pad application is complete, but we are not done with learning about the canvas. Now we'll move on to our next application, Photo Pad, where we will learn about some more advanced canvas features and the File API.

Photo Pad

The next application we are going to write is called Photo Pad. It will look a lot like Canvas Pad, and reuse the same code for the toolbar and menus. But instead of being a drawing application, it will be a photo manipulation application. The user will be able to load images and select from a few different effects, such as invert, black and white, or sepia, to apply to the image.

Time for action – creating Photo Pad

Let's start off, as usual, by copying the application template we created in *Chapter 1*, *The Task at Hand*, and renaming the filenames to `photoPad.html`, `photoPad.css`, and `photoPad.js`. In the HTML file, we will add a toolbar with buttons for Load, Save, and Effects. You can find the code for this section in `Chapter 5/example5.2`:

```
<body>
    <div id="app">
        <header>Photo Pad </header>
        <div id="main">
            <div id="toolbar">
                <div class="dropdown-menu">
                    <button data-action="menu">Load</button>
                    <ul id="load-menu" data-option="file-picker"
                        class="file-picker menu">
                        <li data-value="file-picker">
                            <input type="file" />
                        </li>
                    </ul>
                </div>
                <button data-action="save">Save</button>
                <div class="dropdown-menu">
                    <button data-action="menu">Effects</button>
                    <ul data-option="applyEffect" class="menu">
                        <li data-value="invert">Invert</li>
                    </ul>
                </div>
            </div>
            <canvas width="0" height="0">
                Sorry, your browser doesn't support canvas.
            </canvas>
        </div>
        <footer>Click load to choose a file</footer>
    </div>
</body>
```

The Load toolbar item has a drop-down menu, but instead of menu items it has a file input control in it where the user can select a file to load. The Effects item has a drop-down menu of effects. For now we just have one in there, Invert, but we will add more later.

For our CSS we will copy everything we had in `canvasPad.css` to `photoPad.css`, so that we get all of the same styling for the toolbar and menus. We will also use the `Toolbar` object in `toolbar.js`.

In our JavaScript file we will change the application object name to `PhotoPadApp`. We also need a couple of variables in `PhotoPadApp`. We will set the `canvas` variable to the `<canvas>` element, the `context` variable to the canvas's context, and define an `$img` variable to hold the image we will be showing. Here we initialize it to a new `<img>` element using jQuery:

```
function PhotoPadApp()
{
    var version = "5.2",
        canvas = $("#main>canvas")[0],
        context = canvas.getContext("2d"),
        $img = $("<img>");
```

The first toolbar action we will implement is the **Save** button, since we already have that code from Canvas Pad. We check the action in `toolbarButtonClicked()` to see if it's `"save"`, and if so we get the data URL and open it in a new browser window:

```
function toolbarButtonClicked(action)
{
    switch (action)
    {
        case "save":
            var url = canvas.toDataURL();
            window.open(url, "PhotoPadImage");
            break;
    }
}
```

What just happened?

We created the scaffolding for the Photo Pad application with toolbar items for Load, Save, and Effects. We implemented the save function the same as we did for Canvas Pad.

The next thing we'll implement is the Load drop-down menu since we need an image to manipulate. When the **Load** toolbar button is clicked, it will show the drop-down menu with a file input control in it that we defined previously. All of that we get for free because it's just another drop-down menu in our toolbar.

But before we can do that we need to learn about the HTML5 File API.

The File API

We may not be able to save files directly to the user's filesystem, but we can access files using HTML5's File API. The File API allows you to get information about, and load the contents of, files that the user selects. The user can select files using an input element with a type of `file`. The process for loading a file works in the following way:

1. The user selects one or more files using a `<input type="file">` element.

2. We get the list of files from the input element's `files` property. The list is a `FileList` object containing File objects.

3. You can enumerate over the file list and access the files just like you would an array.

    The `File` object contains three fields.

    ❑   name: This is the filename. It doesn't include path information.

    ❑   size: This is the size of the file in bytes.

    ❑   type: This is the MIME type, if it can be determined.

4. Use a `FileReader` object to read the file's data. The file is loaded asynchronously. After the file has been read, it will call the `onload` event handler. `FileReader` has a number of methods for reading files that take a `File` object and return the file contents.

    ❑   readAsArrayBuffer(): This method reads the file contents into an `ArrayBuffer` object.

    ❑   readAsBinaryString(): This method reads the file contents into a string as binary data.

    ❑   readAsText(): This method reads the file contents into a string as text.

    ❑   readAsDataURL(): This method reads the file contents into a data URL string. You can use this as the URL for loading an image.

Time for action – loading an image file

Let's add some code to the `start()` method of our application to check if the File API is available. You can determine if a browser supports the File API by checking if the `File` and `FileReader` objects exist:

```
this.start = function()
{
    // code not shown...
    if (window.File && window.FileReader)
    {
        $("#load-menu input[type=file]").change(function(e) {
```

```
            onLoadFile($(this));
        });
    }
    else
    {
        loadImage("images/default.jpg");
    }
}
```

First we check if the `File` and `FileReader` objects are available in the `window` object. If
so, we hook up a change event handler for the file input control to call the `onLoadFile()`
method passing in the `<input>` element wrapped in a jQuery object. If the File API is not
available we will just load a default image by calling `loadImage()`, which we will write later.

Let's implement the `onLoadFile()` event handler method:

```
function onLoadFile($input)
{
    var file = $input[0].files[0];
    if (file.type.match("image.*"))
    {
        var reader = new FileReader();
        reader.onload = function() { loadImage(reader.result); };
        reader.readAsDataURL(file);
    }
    else
    {
        alert("Not a valid image type: " + file.type);
        setStatus("Error loading image!");
    }
}
```

Here we get the file that was selected by looking at the file input's `files` array and taking
the first one. Next we check the file type, which is a MIME type, to make sure it is an image.
We are using the `String` object's regular expression `match()` method to check that it starts
with `"image"`.

If it is an image, we create a new instance of the `FileReader` object. Then we set the
`onload` event handler to call the `loadImage()` method, passing in the `FileReader`
object's `result` field, which contains the file's contents. Lastly, we call the `FileReader`
object's `readAsDataURL()` method, passing in the `File` object to start loading the
file asynchronously.

If it isn't an image file, we show an alert dialog box with an error message and show an error
message in the footer by calling `setStatus()`.

Once the file has been read, the `loadImage()` method will be called. Here we will use the data URL we got from the `FileReader` object's `result` field to draw the image into the canvas:

```
function loadImage(url)
{
    setStatus("Loading image");
    $img.attr("src", url);
    $img[0].onload = function()
    {
        // Here "this" is the image
        canvas.width = this.width;
        canvas.height = this.height;
        context.drawImage(this, 0, 0);
        setStatus("Choose an effect");
    }
    $img[0].onerror = function()
    {
        setStatus("Error loading image!");
    }
}
```

First we set the `src` attribute for the image element to the data URL we got after the file was loaded. This will cause the image element to load that new image.

Next we define the `onload` event handler for the image, so that we are notified when the image is loaded. Note that when we are inside the `onload` event handler, `this` points to the `<image>` element. First we change the canvas' width and height to the image's width and height. Then we draw the image on the canvas using the context's `drawImage()` method. It takes the image to draw and the x and y coordinates of where to draw it. In this case we draw it at the top-left corner of the canvas (0, 0).

Lastly, we set an `onerror` event handler for the image. If an error occurs loading the image, we show an error message in the footer.

What just happened?

We learned how to use the File API to load an image file from the user's filesystem. After the image was loaded we resized the canvas to the size of the image and drew the image onto the canvas.

Adding effects

Now let's add some effects to the effects menu. The first one we will implement is a color inverter. It will take the image in the canvas and invert the colors so the image looks like an old film negative (remember those?). We can do this by iterating over every pixel in the image and inverting their colors.

You can get the pixels from the canvas using the context's `getImageData()` method. It gets the pixels for a rectangular area of the canvas. You pass it the position and size of the area:

```
var data = context.getImageData(0, 0, width, height);
```

The `getImageData()` method returns an array of bytes, four for each pixel, that represent each pixel's color. The first byte is the red amount, second is the green amount, third is the blue amount, and fourth is the alpha amount. All values are from 0 to 255. The total number of bytes in the array is *4 * width * height*.

After you get the image data, you can access and change any value in the array that you want. Note that this will only change the image in memory. After changing image data, you can write it back to the canvas using the `putImageData()` method. This method takes parameters for the image data to draw and the position to draw it at.

```
context.putImageData(data, 0, 0);
```

Time for action – the imageEffects object

We will now create a new object called `imageEffects` to encapsulate all of the code for our image effects and put it in a new file, `imageEffects.js`. The `imageEffects` object will be a global static object defined using the revealing module pattern.

 With the revealing module pattern, you define a set of functions in a private scope and then return an anonymous object that reveals which of those methods you want to be public. This works well for defining static objects.

Let's start by defining the `imageEffects` object and adding two helper functions which will remain private. They are used to get and set the image data for the entire canvas:

```
var imageEffects = function()
{
    function getImageData(canvas)
    {
        return canvas.getContext("2d").getImageData(0, 0,
            canvas.width, canvas.height)
    }
```

```
function putImageData(canvas, imageData)
{
    canvas.getContext("2d").putImageData(imageData, 0, 0);
}
```

The `getImageData()` method takes a canvas and returns the image data for the entire canvas. The `putImageData()` method takes a canvas and image data as parameters and puts the image data back into the canvas.

Let's implement our first effect; inverting the colors of an image. The `invert()` method takes the canvas as a parameter. Inverting colors is very simple. We just take each color channel for each pixel and subtract its value from the maximum color value of 255:

```
function invert(canvas)
{
    var imageData = getImageData(canvas);
    var data = imageData.data;
    for (var i = 0; i < data.length; i += 4)
    {
        data[i]   = 255 - data[i];   //red
        data[i+1] = 255 - data[i+1]; //green
        data[i+2] = 255 - data[i+2]; //blue
        //data[i+3] is alpha
    }

    putImageData(canvas, imageData);
}
```

First we get the image data for the canvas and then loop over the bytes, incrementing by four every time because there are four bytes for each pixel. Each color channel value is inverted and set back into the byte. The alpha amount is unchanged. Then we put the image data back onto the canvas.

Now let's finish the `imageEffects` object off. We need to return an anonymous object that defines all of the methods that we want to be public. The only one we have so far is the `invert()` method:

```
return {
    invert: invert
};
}();
```

Notice that we have open and close parenthesis at the end of the function declaration. That immediately executes the function and assigns the anonymous object returned to the `imageEffects` variable. So now we have an `imageEffects` object with an `invert()` public method.

Now we need to hook up our Effects menu items to the `imageEffects` object. We can do this in the `menuItemClicked()` method of `PhotoPadApp`. Previously we gave our menu element a `data-option` custom attribute of `"applyEffect"`. So we will check for that:

```
function menuItemClicked(option, value)
{
    if (option == "applyEffect")
    {
        imageEffects[value](canvas);
    }
}
```

We have given our Invert menu item element a `data-value` custom attribute set to `"invert"`. We will use this to dynamically access the `invert()` method in the `imageEffects` object, just like we did for data binding in *Chapter 3, The Devil is in the Details*. We pass in the `canvas` object as a parameter. For `"invert"`, this is equivalent to calling `imageEffects.invert(canvas)`. We will implement all of our menu items in this way so that they automatically bind to a method in the `imageEffects` object.

What just happened?

We created an `imageEffects` object to hold all of our image effects algorithms. We implemented an effect to invert the colors of an image. We hooked up the Effects menu using custom data attributes to bind the menu items to methods in the `imageEffects` object.

Now let's open up our application in the browser and give it a try. After loading an image, choose **Invert** from the **Effects** menu and you should see the inverted image:

Time for action – black and white

Ok, the `invert()` method was pretty simple. Let's try something a little more challenging, but not much more. We will implement an effect that changes a color image to black and white. Let's implement a `toBlackAnWhite()` method in the `imageEffects` object:

```
function toBlackAndWhite(canvas)
{
    var imageData = getImageData(canvas);
    var data = imageData.data;
    for (var i = 0; i < data.length; i += 4)
    {
        var grayscale = (data[i] * 0.3) +
            (data[i + 1] * .59) +
            (data[i + 2] * .11);
        data[i]   = grayscale;
        data[i+1] = grayscale;
        data[i+2] = grayscale;
    }

    putImageData(canvas, imageData);
}
```

For each pixel, we compute the gray scale value by taking a percentage of each color channel and adding them together; 30 percent red, 59 percent green, and 11 percent blue. Then we set each color channel to that gray scale value.

Now let's add a menu item for black and white to the Effects menu. The `data-value` attribute is set to the method we created previously, `toBlackAndWhite`:

```
<li data-value="toBlackAndWhite">B&amp;W</li>
```

What just happened?

We created a filter to change each pixel to its gray scale value and set it back into the image data. Now we can convert a color image to black and white:

Time for action – sepia

Let's implement another simple effect. This time we will convert the image to sepia, which gives it an old-timey picture look. Sepia is very similar to black and white except a little warmer. First let's add the menu item for it and set the `data-value` attribute to `toSepia`:

```
<li data-value="toSpeia">Sepia</li>
```

Now let's add a `toSepia()` method to the `imageEffects` object.:

```
function toSepia(canvas, depth, intensity)
{
    depth = depth || 20;
    intensity = intensity || 10;

    var imageData = getImageData(canvas);
    var data = imageData.data;
    for (var i = 0; i < data.length; i += 4)
    {
        var grayscale = (data[i] * 0.3) +
            (data[i + 1] * .59) +
```

```
                (data[i + 2] * .11);
        data[i]   = Math.min(255, grayscale + (depth * 2));
        data[i+1] = Math.min(255, grayscale + depth);
        data[i+2] = Math.max(0, grayscale - intensity);
    }

    putImageData(canvas, imageData);
}
```

Although `toSepia()` has three parameters, we will only pass in one parameter, the canvas, so we can use our default Effects menu handling code, and set the rest to default values. The first two lines of the method set default values for the `depth` and `intensity` parameters. `depth` is used to adjust the red and green channels and `intensity` is used to adjust the blue channel to give more fine-tuning over the final result.

To convert a pixel to its sepia tone, we first get the gray scale value the same way as we did for black and white. Then instead of just setting the gray scale for all color channels, we adjust those values based on the channel. Red is boosted the most, which accounts for sepia's reddish tone. Green is also boosted, half as much as red. Blue is reduced by the intensity amount. We use the `Math.max()` and `min()` function to make sure we don't set the value out of range.

What just happened?

We created a filter to convert color images to sepia by finding the gray scale and then adjusting the color channels independently by a fixed amount that can be passed in as parameters or defaulted:

Try using different percentages of red, green, and blue when computing the gray scale value
to see what effect it has on the image. Try passing in different values for depth and intensity
to see what effect it has on the sepia tone.

Image distortion

Next we will add a more advanced effect. We will take the image and distort it with waves
to make it look like a reflection in the water. We can do this using the `Math.sin()` method
to offset the pixel positions from their original positions in a wavy pattern. So instead of
changing color channels, this time we will be moving pixels around.

Time for action – making waves

Let's add the menu item for our wave effect. We give it a `data-value` custom attribute set
to `makeWaves`:

```
<li data-value="makeWaves">Waves</li>
```

Now we will code the `makeWaves()` method. It will take four parameters; `canvas`,
`amplitude`, `frequency`, and `phase`. `amplitude` determines how big the waves will be,
`frequency` determines how many waves there are, and `phase` determines where the
waves begin. Like the `toSepia()` method we will only pass in the `canvas` parameter,
but you can try different parameters to see what effect they have:

```
function makeWaves(canvas, amplitude, frequency, phase)
{
    amplitude = amplitude || 10;
    frequency = frequency || 4;
    phase = phase || 0;

    var data = getImageData(canvas).data;
    var newImageData = getImageData(canvas);
    var newData = newImageData.data;
    var width = newImageData.width;
    var height = newImageData.height;

    // Adjust frequency to height of image
    frequency = frequency * 2 * Math.PI / height;

    for (var y = 0; y < height; y++)
    {
        var xoff = 4 * Math.floor(amplitude *
```

```
            Math.sin(y * frequency + phase));
    var yoff = y * 4 * width;

    for (var x = 0; x < width; x++)
    {
        var pos = yoff + x * 4;
        newData[pos + xoff]     = data[pos];
        newData[pos + xoff + 1] = data[pos+1];
        newData[pos + xoff + 2] = data[pos+2];
        newData[pos + xoff + 3] = data[pos+3];
    }
  }

    putImageData(canvas, newImageData);
}
```

First thing we do is set the default values for the parameters. Then we set up some variables. This time we will need two sets of image data. One is our original image and the other, newImageData, is our working set that we will be changing and eventually write back to the canvas.

Next we adjust the frequency value so it is relative to the height of the image. That way if we want a frequency of four, there will be four waves from top to bottom of the image.

Now it's time to iterate over the pixels. In the outer loop we iterate over the rows of the image. For each row we calculate the x offset by computing the sine value for that row and multiplying it by 4, the number of color channels per pixel. This gives us the offset, in bytes, into the image data array. We also compute the y offset, which is the byte offset into the array for the current row.

Next we iterate over each pixel in the row. Inside this loop we copy the pixel data from the original image data to the working image data array offsetting the positions. Applying the sine wave to get the pixel offsets gives us a wavy pattern:

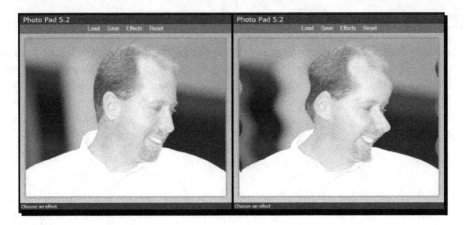

What just happened?

We created a distortion effect that uses a sine wave to make an image look wavy. It does this by computing the offset from the original image and copying the pixels to the new image using the offset.

Have a go hero

Try coming up with your own effect and adding it to the Photo Pad application. For example, you could darken or lighten an image. For a more advanced effect try to blur the image by computing the average color of a pixel and its neighboring pixels (if you want to see how it's done, I've implemented it in the example code for this section).

Pop quiz

Q1. How are touch events different from mouse events?

1. Touch events can have any number of points
2. Touch events don't have any points
3. Touch events don't have a `preventDefault()` method
4. There is no difference

Q2. How many bytes per pixel are there in the canvas image data?

1. One
2. Three
3. Four
4. Eight

Summary

In this chapter we continued working with the Canvas Pad application. We learned about drawing text on the canvas and transformations by drawing an ellipse. We made Canvas Pad touch enabled by adding support for touch events. Then we created a new application called Photo Pad where we learned about loading files from the user's filesystem using the HTML5 File API. We did some image processing to learn how to directly access and manipulate pixels on the canvas.

We covered the following concepts in this chapter:

- How to draw text on the canvas
- How to use the Canvas API transformations to translate, rotate, scale and so on, to change the way things are drawn to the canvas
- How to create a jQuery plugin to check for touch devices and add touch events to elements
- How to use the File API to access files on the user's filesystem and read them into memory using the `FileReader` object
- How to load an image file and draw it into the canvas
- How to access the pixels of the canvas and manipulate their colors to implement some image processing filters

In the next chapter we head off in a whole new direction again. We will learn about the HTML5 `<audio>` element and Audio API by building a virtual piano.

6
Piano Man

"More than art, more than literature, music is universally accessible."
– Billy Joel

In this chapter, we will learn how to use audio by creating a virtual piano application. First, we will learn about the HTML5 Audio element and API. Then we will create an audio manager to load audio files asynchronously and cache them for playback later. We will create a keyboard using HTML elements and style it using CSS.

We will learn the following in this chapter:

- The HTML5 `<audio>` element and its attributes
- How to use the Audio API to control audio in an application
- How to dynamically load audio files
- How to handle keyboard events to turn the computer keyboard into a piano keyboard
- How to use a range input to control the volume of an audio element
- How to check if the range input type is supported by your browser

HTML5 audio overview

Before we start writing our piano application, we need to learn the basics of how to use HTML5 audio. So let's start with an overview of the `<audio>` element and its API.

The HTML5 <audio> element

The HTML5 <audio> element is used to define an audio file to play in your web page or application. The audio element can have visible controls on the page or it can remain hidden and be controlled from JavaScript. Here are a few of the most useful attributes it supports:

- src: URL of the audio file to load.
- autoplay: Used to specify that the file should start playing as soon as it's loaded.
- controls: Tells the browser to display audio controls on the page. Otherwise, nothing is displayed for the element.
- loop: Specifies that the audio will play in a loop.
- muted: Specifies that the audio will be muted.
- preload: Defines how the audio file is loaded.
- auto: Loads the audio file when the page loads. This is the default.
- none: Does not preload the file, waits until it is played.
- metadata: Loads only metadata about the file when the page loads.

The following plays audioFile.mp3 automatically after the page loads and shows the audio controls on the page:

```
<audio src="audioFile.mp3" autoplay controls>
    Your browser doesn't support audio.
</audio>
```

Here's what it looks like when displayed on the page in Chrome:

If the browser doesn't support the <audio> element, it will display whatever content is inside the element.

Although you can specify the file to load using the src attribute, it is not recommended. Different browsers support different file types, so if you only specify one it may not work on all browsers. Instead, you should specify <source> child elements inside the <audio> element to define a list of different audio files to use. The browser will use the first one that it supports:

```
<audio controls>
    <source src="audioFile.mp3">
    <source src="audioFile.ogg">
```

```
        <source src="audioFile.wav">
    </audio>
```

The three primary audio types supported are MP3, Ogg, and WAV. You should at least provide the MP3 and Ogg files, since all of the major browsers support one or the other. If you also want to include a WAV file, put it last in the list since WAV files are not compressed and therefore take a lot of bandwidth to download.

The HTML5 Audio API

If all you could do with HTML5 audio is put an element on a web page to let the user listen to music, it would be pretty boring, and this chapter would be over. But like the `<canvas>` element, the `<audio>` element has a whole API backing it up. We can use the Audio API to control how and when audio clips are played from JavaScript.

The Audio API contains a large number of methods and properties. Here are a few of the most useful ones:

- `play()`: Starts playing the audio clip.
- `pause()`: Pauses playback of the audio clip.
- `canPlayType(type)`: Used to determine if a certain audio type is supported by the browser. Pass in an audio MIME type such as `"audio/ogg"` or `"audio/mpeg"`. It returns one of the following values:
    - `"probably"`: Most likely supports it
    - `"maybe"`: The browser may be able to play it
    - `""` (empty string): Doesn't support it
- `currentTime`: Used to get or set the current playback time in seconds. This allows us to cue up the sound at a certain point before playing it. Usually we will set it to 0 to restart the sound.
- `volume`: Used to get or set the volume. Can be any value between 0 and 1.
- `ended`: Used to determine if the sound has played all the way through.

 Note that the `<audio>` and `<video>` elements both share the same API. So if you know how to use HTML audio, you know how to use video as well.

We can use the Audio API to do some interesting things with sounds. In this chapter, we will create a virtual piano that the user can play on the web page by clicking the keys of a piano keyboard on the screen.

Loading audio files

You could define all of the audio files for your application by adding `<audio>` elements for each one to your HTML file. However, we can also load audio files dynamically from JavaScript to control how and when they are loaded. We can load them just like we loaded image files dynamically in the previous chapter. First, we create a new `<audio>` element and set the `src` attribute to the name of the audio file:

```
var audio = $("<audio>")[0];
audio.src = "2C.mp3";
```

Next, we add an event handler to get notified when the audio file has finished loading. There are two events that we can use. The `canplay` event is fired as soon as the browser has enough data to start playing the audio. The `canplaythrough` event is fired after the file has been completely loaded:

```
audio.addEventListener("canplaythrough", function()
{
    audio.play();
});
```

Time for action – creating an AudioManager object

Let's encapsulate the loading of audio files into a re-usable object. We will create a new object called `AudioManager` and place it in a file named `audioManager.js`. This object will abstract all of the code needed to load, cache, and access audio files.

The constructor for our object takes one parameter named `audioPath`, which is the path to where audio files are stored:

```
function AudioManager(audioPath)
{
    audioPath = audioPath || "";
    var audios = {},
        audioExt = getSupportedFileTypeExt();
```

If `audioPath` isn't defined, we default it to an empty string. Then we add a variable named `audios` which is an object that will be used to cache all of the `<audio>` elements that are loaded. Finally, we define a variable to hold the audio file extension supported by the browser, which we will determine by calling the `getSupportedFileTypeExt()` method:

```
function getSupportedFileTypeExt()
{
    var audio = $("<audio>")[0];
    if (audio.canPlayType("audio/ogg")) return ".ogg";
    if (audio.canPlayType("audio/mpeg")) return ".mp3";
```

```
        if (audio.canPlayType("audio/wav")) return ".wav";
        return "";
    };
```

First, we create a new <audio> element in memory and use that to call the `canPlayType()` method to determine the file type the browser supports. Then we return the file extension for that type.

Next, we need a way to get the audio files from the `AudioManager` object. Let's add a public `getAudio()` method:

```
    this.getAudio = function(name, onLoaded, onError)
    {
        var audio = audios[name];
        if (!audio)
        {
            audio = createAudio(name, onLoaded, onError);
            // Add to cache
            audios[name] = audio;
        }
        else if (onLoaded)
        {
            onLoaded(audio);
        }
        return audio;
    };
```

The `getAudio()` method takes three parameters. The first is the name of the audio file without the extension. We will add the audio path and default extension to it later when loading the file. The next two parameters are optional. The second parameter is a function that will get called when the file has finished loading. The third is a function that will get called if there was an error loading the file.

The first thing `getAudio()` does is check the `audios` object to see if we already loaded and cached that file. The `audios` object is used like an associative array in this case, where the key is the filename and the value is the audio element. This makes it easy to look up <audio> elements by name.

If the file hasn't been added to the cache yet, then we create a new `audio` element and load it by calling the `createAudio()` method, which we will implement next. Then it adds the new element to the `audios` object to cache it.

If the filename was already in the cache, then we immediately call the `onLoaded()` handler function that was passed in as a parameter since the file has been loaded.

Now let's write the private `createAudio()` method. It takes the same parameters as the previous method:

```
function createAudio(name, onLoaded, onError)
{
    var audio = $("<audio>")[0];
    audio.addEventListener("canplaythrough", function()
    {
        if (onLoaded) onLoaded(audio);
        audio.removeEventListener("canplaythrough",
            arguments.callee);
    });
    audio.onerror = function()
    {
        if (onError) onError(audio);
    };
    audio.src = audioPath + "/" + name + audioExt;
    return audio;
}
}
```

First, we create a new `<audio>` element using jQuery. Then we add an event listener for `canplaythrough`. When the event is fired, we check if an `onLoaded` function was passed into the method. If so, we call it passing it the new `<audio>` element. We also need to remove the event listener because some browsers will call it every time the audio is played.

We also add an `onerror` handler to the `<audio>` element to check for errors while loading the file. If we get an error, it calls the `onError` function, if it was defined.

Next, we set the `src` attribute of the `<audio>` element to the URL of the audio file. We build the URL by combining `audioPath`, the name parameter, and `audioExt`. This will cause the audio file to start loading. Finally, we return the new `<audio>` element.

What just happened?

We created an object called `AudioManager` to load and cache audio files. The first time we request an audio file, it gets loaded and cached. The next time it uses the cached audio. For example, if our browser supports Ogg files, the following code will load the `audio/2C.ogg` audio file:

```
var audioManager = new AudioManager("audio");
var audio = audioManager.getAudio("2C");
```

HTML5 piano application

Now let's create our HTML5 piano application. We will have two octaves worth of piano keys, both black and white, and we will use some styling to make it look like a real keyboard. When the user clicks on a key with the mouse, it will play the corresponding note, which is defined in an audio file.

You can find the code for this section in chapter6/example6.1.

Time for action – creating a virtual piano

We'll start as usual by copying our application template that we created in *Chapter 1, The Task at Hand*, and renaming the files to piano.html, piano.css, and piano.js. We also need touchEvents.js that we created in the previous chapter.

Inside piano.js, we'll change the application object to PianoApp:

```
function PianoApp()
{
    var version = "6.1",
        audioManager = new AudioManager("audio");
```

We create an instance of AudioManager and pass in the path to our audio files, which will be the audio folder. Now let's open our HTML file and add all of the piano keys:

```
<div id="keyboard">
    <div id="backboard"></div>
    <div class="keys">
        <div data-note="2C" class="piano-key white"></div>
        <div data-note="2C#" class="piano-key black"></div>
        <div data-note="2D" class="piano-key white"></div>
        <div data-note="2D#" class="piano-key black"></div>
        <div data-note="2E" class="piano-key white"></div>
        <div data-note="2F" class="piano-key white"></div>
        <div data-note="2F#" class="piano-key black"></div>
        <div data-note="2G" class="piano-key white"></div>
        <div data-note="2G#" class="piano-key black"></div>
        <div data-note="2A" class="piano-key white"></div>
        <div data-note="2A#" class="piano-key black"></div>
        <div data-note="2B" class="piano-key white"></div>
        <!-- third octave not shown -->
        <div data-note="4C" class="piano-key white"></div>
    </div>
</div>
```

Inside of the "main" element, we add a `<div>` tag with `id` set to `keyboard`. Inside there we have a `<div>` tag that will be the backboard and a `<div>` tag that will contain all of the keys. Each key is defined by an element that contains a class of `piano-key` and a class of either `white` or `black` depending on the key color. Each key element also has a `data-note` custom data attribute. This will be set to the name of the piano key's note and will also be the name of the matching audio file.

Our piano has two full octaves of piano keys. Each key has its own audio file. Since each octave has 12 notes, and we have one more C note at the end of the keyboard, we will have 25 audio files named `2C` through `4C`. We want to supply audio files in both Ogg and MP3 formats to support all browsers, so in all we have 50 audio files:

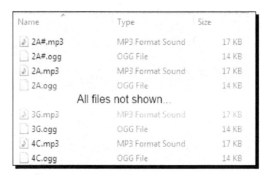

Name	Type	Size
2A#.mp3	MP3 Format Sound	17 KB
2A#.ogg	OGG File	14 KB
2A.mp3	MP3 Format Sound	17 KB
2A.ogg	OGG File	14 KB
All files not shown...		
3G.mp3	MP3 Format Sound	17 KB
3G.ogg	OGG File	14 KB
4C.mp3	MP3 Format Sound	17 KB
4C.ogg	OGG File	14 KB

Let's open `piano.css` and style the application. First of all we'll make the application take up the whole browser window by setting `position` to `absolute` and setting all of the `position` values to `0`. We'll give it a linear gradient from white to blue:

```
#app
{
    position: absolute;
    top: 0;
    bottom: 0;
    left: 0;
    right: 0;
    margin: 4px;
    background-color: #999;
    /* browser specific gradients not shown */
    background: linear-gradient(top, white, #003);
}
```

We also set the `footer` selector's `position` attribute to `absolute` and `bottom` to `0`, so it hugs the bottom of the window:

```
#app>footer
{
```

```
        position: absolute;
        bottom: 0;
        padding: 0.25em;
        color: WhiteSmoke;
    }
```

In the main section, we set `text-align` to `center`, so the keyboard is centered on the page:

```
#main
{
    padding: 4px;
    text-align: center;
}
```

Now let's style the keyboard to make it look like a real piano keyboard. First, we give the entire keyboard a gradient from dark brown to light brown and a shadow to give it some depth:

```
#keyboard
{
    padding-bottom: 6px;
    background-color: saddlebrown;
    /* browser specific gradients not shown */
    background: linear-gradient(top, #2A1506, saddlebrown);
    box-shadow: 3px 3px 4px 1px rgba(0, 0, 0, 0.9);
}
```

Next, we style the backboard, which hides the tops of the keys. We give it a dark brown color, make it `32` pixels high, and give it a shadow to add depth. In order to get the shadow to draw over the piano keys, we need to set `position` as `relative`:

```
#backboard
{
    position: relative;
    height: 32px;
    background-color: #2A1506;
    border-bottom: 2px solid black;
    box-shadow: 3px 3px 4px 1px rgba(0, 0, 0, 0.9);
}
```

All of the piano keys share some base styling that is defined with the `piano-key` class. First, we set `display` as `inline-block` so they stay on the same line and also have width and height. Then we give the bottom a border radius to make them look rounded. We'll also set the `cursor` property to `pointer` so the user gets an indication that they can be clicked:

```
#keyboard .piano-key
{
    display: inline-block;
    border-bottom-right-radius: 4px;
    border-bottom-left-radius: 4px;
    cursor: pointer;
}
```

Finally, we get to the black and white keys' styles. The white keys are a little wider and taller than the black keys. We also give them an ivory color and a shadow. Lastly, we need to set `z-index` to 1, because they need to be displayed behind the black keys:

```
#keyboard .piano-key.white
{
    width: 50px;
    height: 300px;
    background-color: Ivory;
    box-shadow: 3px 3px 4px 1px rgba(0, 0, 0, 0.7);
    z-index: 1;
}
```

The black keys are a little smaller than the white. In order to make the black keys show over top of the white keys, we give set `z-index` to 2. To make them seem to be in between the white keys, we set their `position` properties to `relative` and use a negative `left` offset to move them over top of the white keys. We also need a negative `right-margin` value, so the next white key gets pulled over and under it:

```
#keyboard .piano-key.black
{
    position: relative;
    width: 40px;
    height: 200px;
    left: -23px;
    margin-right: -46px;
    vertical-align: top;
    background-color: black;
    box-shadow: 2px 2px 3px 1px rgba(0, 0, 0, 0.6);
    z-index: 2;
}
```

This is how our piano would look:

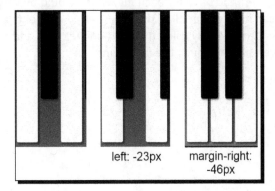

The first image shows the keys with no margins set. Doesn't look much like a real keyboard, does it? The next image shows what it looks like with the `left` margin set. It's getting better but the white key hasn't moved over. Setting the right margin takes care of that.

What just happened?

We created a new HTML5 piano application starting with our application template. We defined all of the keys in HTML and then we styled them using negative offsets and margins to make the keys line up like a real keyboard.

There you have it! We now have a two octave keyboard that looks pretty darn realistic:

Time for action – loading the notes

We have a keyboard but there's no sound yet. Let's head back over to our JavaScript and load all of the audio files. We will create a new method called `loadAudio()` and call it from the application's `start()` method.

There are two ways by which we could load all the files. We could load them one at a time by calling `audioManager.getAudio()` for each file, which would be very verbose and require a lot of typing. Or we can iterate over all of the `piano-key` elements and get the filename from their `data-note` attributes. By using this method we could add more piano keys to the HTML and wouldn't even have to touch the JavaScript:

```javascript
function loadAudio()
{
    var count = 0,
        loaded = 0,
        error = false;

    $(".keyboard .piano-key").each(function()
    {
        count++;
        var noteName = escape($(this).data("note"));
        audioManager.getAudio(noteName,
            function()
            {
                if (error) return;
                if (++loaded == count) setStatus("Ready.");
                else setStatus("Loading " +
                        Math.floor(100 * loaded / count) + "%");
            },
            function(audio)
            {
                error = true;
                setStatus("Error loading: " + audio.src);
            }
        );
    });
}
```

The first thing we do is define some variables to keep track of the number of audio files that are being loaded and the number that have been loaded. We will use those to calculate the percent complete. We also need a variable to set if we get an error loading a file.

The next thing we do is select all of the `piano-key` elements using jQuery and call `each()` to iterate over them. For each one we do the following:

1. Add 1 to the `count` variable to keep track of the total number of files.

2. Get the note name, which is also the filename, from the `data-note` attribute. Notice that we must use the `escape()` function because some notes contain the sharp sign #, which is illegal in a URL.

3. Call `audioManager.getAudio()` passing in the note name. This will cause the audio file to get loaded and cached. The next time we call `getAudio()` for this note, it will be loaded and ready to play.

4. The second parameter to `getAudio()` is a function that gets called when each file has finished loading successfully. In this function we increment the loaded variable. Then we check if all of the files have been loaded and if so, show a ready message. Otherwise, we compute the percent complete of loaded files and show it in the footer by calling `setStatus()`.

5. The last parameter to `getAudio()` is a function that gets called if there is an error loading a file. When that happens, we set the `error` variable to `true` and display a message showing the file that couldn't be loaded.

 Note that if you are running this application through a web server such as IIS, you may need to add the `.ogg` file type to the list of MIME types for your site (`.ogg, audio/ogg`). Otherwise, you will get an error saying that the file is not found.

What just happened?

We used the `AudioManager` object to load all of the sounds for each keyboard key dynamically using their `data-note` attributes as the filename. Now we have all of our audio files loaded, cached, and ready to play.

Time for action – playing the notes

The next thing we need to do is add event handlers to play an `<audio>` element when a piano key is clicked or touched. We will hook up and event handlers to all of our piano keys and play the associated note when they are fired.

 At the time of this writing, the state of audio on mobile devices isn't very good. Although a touch device would be perfect for a piano app, the sounds don't always play correctly because of the way mobile browsers cache audio (or not).

Let's create a method called `initKeyboard()` that will be called from the application's `start()` method:

```
function initKeyboard()
{
    var $keys = $(".keyboard .piano-key");
    if ($.isTouchSupported)
    {
```

```
        $keys.touchstart(function(e) {
            e.stopPropagation();
            e.preventDefault();
            keyDown($(this));
        })
        .touchend(function() { keyUp($(this)); })
    }
    else
    {
        $keys.mousedown(function() {
            keyDown($(this));
            return false;
        })
        .mouseup(function() { keyUp($(this)); })
        .mouseleave(function() { keyUp($(this)); });
    }
}
```

First, we use jQuery to select all of the `piano-key` elements on the keyboard. Then, we use the touch event's jQuery extension to check if the browser supports touch events. If so, we hook up touch event handlers to the piano keys. Otherwise, we hook up the mouse event handlers.

When a key is touched or the mouse clicked down, it calls the `keyDown()` method passing in the key element wrapped in a jQuery object.

 Note that in this context, `this` is the element that was clicked. When the key is untouched or the mouse released, or the mouse leaves the element, we call the `keyUp()` method.

Let's write the `keyDown()` method first:

```
function keyDown($key)
{
    if (!$key.hasClass("down"))
    {
        $key.addClass("down");
        var noteName = $key.data("note");
        var audio = audioManager.getAudio(escape(noteName));
        audio.currentTime = 0;
        audio.play();
    }
}
```

In the `keyDown()` method we first check if the key is already pressed down by checking if it has a class of `down`. If not, we add a class of `down` to the key element. We will use this to style the key to make it look like it's pressed. Then, we get the key's note name from the `data-note` custom attribute. We pass that to the `audioManager.getAudio()` method to get the `<audio>` element. To start playing the audio clip, we first set the `currentTime` property to `0` to cue up the sound at the start. Then we call the Audio API's `play()` method to start playing it.

```
function keyUp($key)
{
    $key.removeClass("down");
}
```

The `keyUp()` method simply removes the `down` class from the element, so the key won't be styled in the down position any more.

The last thing we need to do is add the styling for the key down state. We will use a gradient to make it look like the end of the key is pressed down. We also make the shadow a little smaller since the key is not as high when pressed:

```
.keyboard .piano-key.white.down
{
    background-color: #F1F1F0;
    /* Browser-specific gradients not shown */
    background: linear-gradient(top, Ivory, #D5D5D0);
    box-shadow: 2px 2px 3px 1px rgba(0, 0, 0, 0.6);
}
.keyboard .piano-key.black.down
{
    background-color: #111;
    /* Browser-specific gradients not shown */
    background: linear-gradient(top, Black, #222);
    box-shadow: 1px 1px 2px 1px rgba(0, 0, 0, 0.6);
}
```

What just happened?

We hooked up event handlers to the piano keys to play the associated notes when they are clicked with the mouse or touched on a touch device. We added some styling to give a visual indication that the key is pressed down. Now we have a functioning piano using HTML5 Audio. Go ahead and open it in your browser and bang out some tunes.

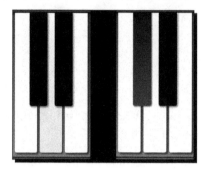

Keyboard events

Using the mouse to play notes on our piano works okay, but it would be better if we could play more than one note at a time. To do that, we can use the computer's keyboard to play notes. To do this we will add keyboard event handlers to the DOM `document` in JavaScript and map keyboard keys to piano keys.

The top two rows of the keyboard will be used for the first octave and the bottom two for the second octave. For example, pressing the *Q* key will play the lowest C note. Pressing the *2* key will play C#, *W* will play D, and so on. For the second octave, pressing *Z* will play middle C, *S* will play C#, and so on:

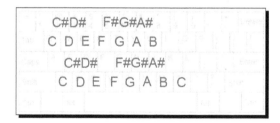

You can find the code for this section in `chapter6/example6.2`.

Time for action – adding keyboard events

The first thing we need to do is add `keycodes.js` to our application. This file contains a global static object named `keyCodes` that maps keys on the keyboard to their associated key code. For example, `keyCodes.ENTER` is equal to `13`. Using this will make our code more readable than using key code numbers.

The next thing we need to do is open the HTML and add a new custom data attribute to the `piano-key` elements. We will call it `data-keycode` and it will be set to the value in the `keyCode` object we want to associate with the piano key:

```
<div data-note="2C" data-keycode="Q" class="piano-key white"
title="C2"></div>
<!—elements not shown -->
<div data-note="4C" data-keycode="COMMA" class="piano-key white"
title="C4"></div>
```

Now we need to map key codes to the notes. We will add an object to our application called `keyCodesToNotes` to hold our mappings. We will initialize it in the `initKeyboard()` method:

```
function initKeyboard()
{
    // Code not shown...
    $keys.each(function() {
        var $key = $(this);
        var keyCode = keyCodes[$key.data("keycode")];
        keyCodesToNotes[keyCode] = $key.data("note");
    });
}
```

Here, we iterate over all `piano-key` elements, getting the `data-keycode` custom attribute for each one and using that to get the key code from the `keyCodes` object. Then we add the mapping to `keyCodesToNotes` by setting it to the element's `data-note` custom attribute. For example, the key code for the *Q* key is 81 and the associated piano key note is 2C. So `keyCodesToNotes[81]` will be set to 2C.

Now let's add the keyboard event handlers. When checking for key down, up, or pressed events, you need to attach your event handlers to the HTML document. Let's add `keydown` and `keyup` event handlers in the `start()` method of our application:

```
this.start = function()
{
  // Code not shown...
    $(document).keydown(onKeyDown)
               .keyup(onKeyUp);
}
```

The `keydown` event handler calls the `onKeyDown()` method. The `keyup` handler calls `onKeyUp()`:

```
function onKeyDown(e)
{
    var note = keyCodesToNotes[e.which];
    if (note)
    {
        pressPianoKey(note);
    }
}
```

In the `onKeyDown()` method we look up the note for the key that was pressed using the `keyCodesToNotes` object. jQuery defines a `which` field on the key event object that contains the key code. If the key code matched to a note on our keyboard, then we call the `pressPianoKey()` method passing it the `note` parameter:

```
function onKeyUp(e)
{
    var note = keyCodesToNotes[e.which];
    if (note)
    {
        releasePianoKey(note);
    }
}
```

The `onKeyUp()` method works the same way except that we call the `releasePianoKey()` method.

```
function pressPianoKey(note)
{
    var $key = getPianoKeyElement(note);
    keyDown($key);
}
```

In the `pressPianoKey()` method, we get the name of the note to play as a parameter. Then we call `getPianoKeyElement()` to get the piano key element associated with that note. Finally, we pass that element into the `keyDown()` method that we already implemented when we added mouse and touch events. In this way, we simulate the user clicking a piano key element on the screen.

```
function releasePianoKey(note)
{
    var $key = getPianoKeyElement(note);
    keyUp($key);
}
```

The `releasePianoKey()` method works exactly the same way except it calls the existing `keyUp()` method.

```
function getPianoKeyElement(note)
{
    return $(".keyboard .piano-key[data-note=" + note + "]");
}
```

In the `getPianoKeyElement()` method, we find the `piano-key` element associated with a note by using a jQuery select matching on the `data-note` custom attribute.

What just happened?

We added keyboard key event handlers to the HTML document of our application. We mapped the key codes when a key is pressed to a piano key, so that the user can press keys on the keyboard to play the piano. By passing the `piano-key` element into `keyDown()` and `keyUp()`, we simulate the user clicking on those keys. They get the `down` class added to them so it looks like they are really being pressed.

Check it out for yourself. Try pressing two or three keys at a time and play some chords.

Volume and sustain controls

Let's add some controls to our piano to allow the user to change the volume and sustain. As you may recall, the volume of an `audio` element may be set to any value from 0 to 1.0. We will use a range input control that allows the user to control that via a slider.

The sustain control allows a note to remain playing after the piano key is released. When sustain is turned off, the note will stop playing as soon as the key is released. We will add a checkbox to turn this off and on.

You can find the source code for this section in `chapter6/example6.3`.

Time for action – adding a sustain control

Let's go ahead and add a sustain control to the application. We will use a checkbox input control to turn sustain on and off. In our HTML file, we will add a new `<div>` element with a class of `controls` under the keyboard to hold our controls:

```
<div id="main">
    <!-- keyboard not shown... -->
    <div class="controls">
        <label for="sustain">Sustain: </label>
        <input type="checkbox" id="sustain" checked /><br />
```

```
        </div>
    </div>
```

We define a label and a checkbox with an `id` attribute of `sustain`. We also set it checked by default.

Now let's implement the code for the checkbox in our `PianoApp` application object. First, we need to add a variable named `sustain` and set it to `true`:

```
function PianoApp()
{
    var version = "6.3",
    // Code not shown...
    sustain = true;
```

Next, we hook up a `change` event handler to get notified when the checkbox changes. We will do this in the application's `start()` method:

```
$("#sustain").change(function() { sustain = $(this).is(":checked");
});
```

When the checkbox changes, we figure out if it is checked using the jQuery `is()` filter method passing it the `:checked` filter. If it is checked, the `sustain` variable gets set to true.

Now we need to make some changes to the `keyUp()` method. All the method does now is to remove the `down` class from the `piano-key` element. We need to add code to check the `sustain` variable and stop the sound from playing if this variable is set to `true`:

```
function keyUp($key)
{
    $key.removeClass("down");
    if (!sustain)
    {
        var noteName = $key.data("note");
        var audio = audioManager.getAudio(escape(noteName));
        audio.pause();
    }
}
```

After removing the `down` class, we check the `sustain` variable. If sustain is not set, we get the note name from the `piano-key` element's `data-note` custom attribute and use that to get the `<audio>` element from the `audioManager` object. Then we call the `pause()` method to stop playing the sound.

What just happened?

We added a checkbox to allow the user to turn the sustain control on and off. When sustain is off and the user releases a piano key, we call the Audio API's `pause()` method to stop playback of the note.

Time for action – adding a volume control

Going back into the HTML, let's add a range input control to allow the user to change the volume. We will put it right under the sustain label and control we just added:

```
<label for="volume">Volume: </label>
<input type="range" id="volume" min="1" max="100" value="100" step="1" />
```

We define a label and a range input with an `id` attribute of `volume`. We set the range of the control from `1` to `100` with a `step` value of `1`. We also default the value to `100`.

Back in our `PianoApp` object we add another global variable named `volume` and set it to `1.0`, the maximum volume, by default:

```
function PianoApp()
{
    var version = "6.3",
    // Code not shown...
    sustain = true,
    volume = 1.0;
```

Like the `sustain` checkbox, we need to add a `change` event handler to the `start()` method of our application for the range control:

```
$("#volume").change(function() {

    volume = parseInt($(this).val()) / 100;

});
```

You may have noticed that our range input control has a range of `1` to `100`, while the volume of an `audio` element is defined from `0` to `1.0`. Therefore, in our event handler, we set the `volume` variable to the value of the range control divided by 100.

Now all we need to do is add one line of code to the `keyDown()` method to set the `volume` property of the `audio` element before playing it:

```
audio.currentTime = 0;
audio.volume = volume;
audio.play();
```

```
.controls
{
    margin-top: 2em;
    color: white;
}
.controls input
{
    vertical-align: middle;
}
.controls input[type=range]
{
    width: 10em;
}
```

We set the top margin to give the controls a little breathing room, set vertical align for the controls so labels line up in the middle, and set the width of the volume range control.

There's one more thing we should do to make our application more dynamic. The range input control isn't widely supported by all browsers, so let's add some code to check if it's supported. We'll add an `isInputTypeSupported()` method:

```
function isInputTypeSupported(type)
{
    var $test = $("<input>");
    // Set input element to the type we're testing for
    $test.attr("type", type);
    return ($test[0].type == type);
}
```

First, we create a new `<input>` element in memory. Then we set the `type` attribute to the type we are testing. In our case, that will be `range`. Then we check the `type` attribute to see if it is stuck. If the element retains that type, then the browser supports it.

In the `start()` method we'll add a check for the range type. If you recall from *Chapter 3, The Devil is in the Details*, that if an input type isn't supported, it will just be displayed as a text input field. So if the range type isn't supported, we'll change the width of the field to make it smaller. We don't want a text input field that's `10em` wide to input a number from `0` to `100`:

```
if (!isInputTypeSupported("range")) $("#volume").css("width", "3em");
```

What just happened?

We added a range input control to allow the user to change the volume of the sounds with a slider. Before playing the sound, we set the volume to the value selected by the user. We also wrote a method to check if certain HTML5 input types are supported by the browser. The following is what we have created:

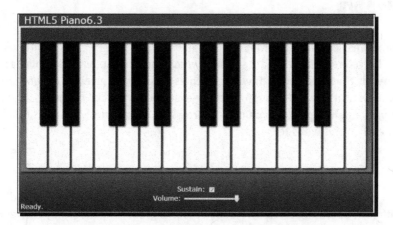

Have a go hero

Create a wrapper object for `<audio>` elements that takes the element as a constructor and contains public methods to access the Audio API methods. Add some convenience methods, for example, `rewind()`, which sets `audio.currentTime = 0`, or `stop()`, which calls `pause()` and `rewind()`.

Pop quiz

Q1. What audio type does the `<audio>` element support?

1. Ogg
2. MP3
3. Wav
4. All of the above

Q2. Which object do you attach keyboard events to?

1. `window`
2. `document`
3. `div`
4. `audio`

Audio tools

Before we leave this chapter, I would like to tell you about a couple of free audio tools that you can use to get and manipulate audio files for your applications.

FreeSound.org

`FreeSound.org` is a website from where you can get audio files that are released under Creative Commons licenses. That means you can use them free of charge with various usage restrictions. There are public domain sounds, which you can use without doing anything. There are sounds that you can do anything with as long as you give the author credit. And there are sounds that you can use for anything except commercial purposes. The FreeSound database is vast and has great searching and browsing capabilities. You can find almost any sound you need on this website.

Audacity

Audacity is a free open source audio editor for recording, slicing, and mixing audio that runs on many different operating systems. Audacity works great for converting between multiple file types, which is great for us since we need to support different audio types for different browsers. It supports all of the main audio types used by the major web browsers, including Ogg, MP3 and WAV.

Summary

In this chapter, we learned how to use the HTML5 `audio` element and API to add sounds to web applications. We saw how to load and cache audio files by creating a re-usable audio manager object. Then we used HTML5 audio to create a virtual piano application for playing the piano in a web page. We used keyboard events to allow the user to play the piano keys via the keyboard. We added controls to change the volume and sustain notes.

We covered the following concepts in this chapter:

- How to add the HTML5 `<audio>` element to a web page and use its attributes to control it
- Using the Audio API from JavaScript to programmatically control the playback of an audio element
- How to load audio files and cache them for playback later
- How to play, pause, and reset an audio file
- How to hook up keyboard events to the document and handle them in our applications
- How to change the volume of an `audio` element using a range input control
- How to check if any HTML5 input type is supported by the browser

In the next chapter, we will take our piano application and turn it into a game called Piano Hero. We will learn about timing, animating elements, and playing back music by creating an audio sequencer.

7
Piano Hero

"One good thing about music, when it hits you, you feel no pain."

— Bob Marley

In this chapter we will turn the piano application from the previous chapter into a game where the player must play the notes of a song at the correct time as they fall down the screen. We will create a splash page that keeps track of image loading and allows the player to choose game options. We will create an audio sequencer to play the songs from music data. During the game we will collect piano keyboard input and validate it to determine the player's score.

We will learn the following in this chapter:

◆ How to use an HTML5 progress bar element to track the loading of resources

◆ How to use JavaScript timers to control playback of audio to play songs

◆ How to animate DOM elements to move them around the screen

◆ How to transition between game states

◆ How to get user input and verify it

Creating Piano Hero

Our Piano Hero game will start with the HTML5 piano application we built in the previous chapter. We will add an audio sequencer to it to play prerecorded songs. To score points, the player will need to follow along and play the notes of the song at the correct time. There will also be a practice mode that just plays the song so the player can hear it.

Our game will have two different main panels. The first will be the splash panel, which is the starting point of the game. When the application first starts, it will display a progress bar as the audio loads. When loading is complete, it will show the options for playing the game. When the player clicks on the play button they will transition to the game panel.

The game panel contains the piano keyboard and an area that shows the notes to play dropping down from above it. If the user plays the correct note at the correct time, they get points. At the end of the song, the player's score and some statistics are displayed. When the game is done, the application will transition back to the splash panel where the user can select options and play again.

It's often helpful to draw a flowchart that shows how the game transitions from one state to another.

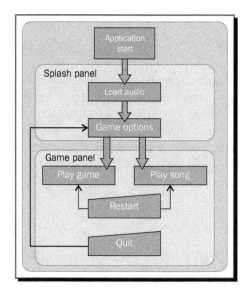

Time for action – creating the splash panel

Let's start by copying the piano application that we created in the previous chapter, and renaming the files to `pinaoHero.html`, `pianoHero.js`, and `pianoHero.css`. We will also rename the main application object to `PianoHeroApp`. You can find the code for this section in `Chapter 7/example7.1`.

Now let's create the splash panel. First we'll define the HTML in `pianoHero.html`. We will add a new `<div>` element above the keyboard element to hold the splash panel:

```
<div id="splash">
    <h1>Piano Hero</h1>
    <section class="loading">
```

```
        Loading audio...<br/>
        <progress max="100" value="0"></progress>
    </section>
```

First we add a section with a class of `"loading"` that displays the status of loading the audio when the application first starts up. Notice that we are using the new HTML5 `<progress>` element. This element is used to implement a progress bar in your application. It has a `max` attribute that defines the maximum value, and a `value` attribute to set the current value. Since we are showing percent complete we set the `max` to `100`. We will update the `value` attribute from JavaScript as audio files are loaded.

Then we add a section with a class of `"error"` that will show an error message if there is an error loading the audio. Otherwise it will be hidden:

```
<section class="error">
    There was an error loading the audio.
</section>
```

Lastly, we add a section that shows the game options and buttons. This panel is shown after all audio has been loaded:

```
<section class="loaded hidden">
    <label>Choose a song</label>
    <select id="select-song">
        <option value="rowBoat">Row Your Boat</option>
        <option value="littleStar">
          Twinkle, Twinkle, Little Star</option>
        <option value="londonBridge">London Bridge</option>
        <option value="furElise">Fur Elise</option>
    </select><br/>
    <label>Choose difficulty</label>
    <select id="select-rate">
        <option value="0.5">Slow (60bpm)</option>
        <option value="1" selected>Normal (120bpm)</option>
        <option value="1.5">Fast (180bpm)</option>
    </select>
    <p>
        <button id="start-game">Start Game</button>
        <button id="start-song">Play Song</button>
    </p>
</section>
</div>
```

Here the user selects the song and difficulty from the drop-down lists. The difficulty is expressed in terms of the rate of speed that the song plays. A value of one is the default speed of 120 beats per minute. A value less than one is slower, and more than one is faster.

Now we need to style the splash panel. Please see the source code for all of the styles. The one noteworthy piece of styling is for the **PIANO HERO** title, which we placed inside an <h1> header element:

```
#splash h1
{
    font-size: 6em;
    color: #003;
    text-transform: uppercase;
    text-shadow: 3px 3px 0px #fff, 5px 5px 0px #003;
}
```

We set the color for the text to dark blue. Then we use text-shadow to produce an interesting block text effect. When using text-shadow, you may specify any number of shadows separated by commas. The shadows will be drawn in order from last to first. So in this case, we first draw a dark blue shadow with an offset of 5 pixels, then a white shadow with an offset of 3 pixels, and finally the dark blue text will be drawn on top of that:

Now let's create a new JavaScript file named splashPanel.js, and define a new object called SplashPanel in it that will contain all of the code to control the splash panel. The constructor will take one parameter, a reference to audioManager:

```
function SplashPanel(audioManager)
{
    var $div = $("#splash"),
    error = false;
```

We define a $div object to hold a reference to the splash panel's root <div> element, and an error variable to set if there was an error loading the audio. Next we define the public show() and hide() methods. These will be called by the main application object to show or hide the panel:

```
    this.show = function()
    {
```

```
        $div.fadeIn();
        return this;
    };
    this.hide = function()
    {
        $div.hide();
        return this;
    };
}
```

Next we will move the `loadAudio()` method from `PianoHeroApp` to `SplashPanel`. In this method we need to make a couple of minor changes to the call to `audioManager.getAudio()`:

```
audioManager.getAudio(noteName,
    function()
    {
        if (error) return;
        if (++loaded == count) showOptions();
        else updateProgress(loaded, count);
    },
    function(audio) { showError(audio); }
);
```

In our function that gets called each time an audio file is loaded, we first check if there was an error, and if so get it out. Then we check if all of the audio files have been loaded (`loaded == count`), and if so call the `showOptions()` method. Otherwise we call the `updateProgress()` method to update the progress bar:

```
function updateProgress(loadedCount, totalCount)
{
    var pctComplete = parseInt(100 * loadedCount / totalCount);
    $("progress", $div)
        .val(pctComplete)
        .text(pctComplete + "%");
}
```

The `updateProgress()` method takes the loaded count and total count as parameters. We compute the percent complete and use that to update the value of the `<progress>` element. We also set the inner text of the `<progress>` element. This will only show for browsers that don't support the `<progress>` element.

```
function showOptions()
{
    $(".loading", $div).hide();
    $(".options", $div).fadeIn();
}
```

The showOptions() method is called after all audio has been loaded. First we hide the element with the "loading" class, and then fade in the element with the "options" class. This hides the progress section and shows the section that contains the game options.

Our error handler function calls showError(), passing it the audio element that failed:

```
function showError(audio)
{
    error = true;
    $(".loading", $div).hide();
    $(".error", $div)
        .append("<div>" + audio.src + "<div>")
        .show();
}
```

In the showError() method we set the error flag to true so we know not to continue in the getAudio() call. First we hide the loading section, then we append the name of the file that failed to the error message, and show the error section.

The last thing we need in our splash panel is to hook up event handlers to the buttons. There are two buttons, **Start Game** and **Play Song**. The only difference between them is that the **Play Song** button plays the song without scoring, so the user can hear the song and practice:

```
$(".options button", $div).click(function()
{
    var songName = $("#select-song>option:selected", $div).val();
    var rate = Number($("#select-rate>option:selected", $div).val());
    var playGame = ($(this).attr("id") == "start-game");
    app.startGame(songName, rate, playGame);
});
```

We use the same event handler for both buttons. First we get the options that the user selected, including the song and playback rate. You can find the selected <option> element in jQuery using the :selected selector. We determine which button the user pressed by looking at the button's id attribute. Then we call the startGame() method on the global app object passing in the selected options. We will write that method later.

What just happened?

We created a splash panel that shows the loading progress of the audio files using an HTML5 `<progress>` element. When it is finished it shows the game options, and then waits for the user to select options and start the game.

Time for action – creating the game panel

The next thing we will create is the game panel. We already have the piano keyboard, which will be part of it. We also need an area above it to show the notes dropping down, and a place to show the results when the game has finished. Let's add these to our HTML file inside the `game` element and above the keyboard:

```
<div id="game">
    <div id="notes-panel">
        <div class="title">PIANO HERO</div>
    </div>
```

The `<div id="notes-panel">` element will be used to hold the elements that represent the notes to play. It is empty for now. The `note` elements will be added dynamically to this element while the game is playing. It has a `<div>` element with the title in it that will show up behind the notes.

```
        <div id="results-panel">
            <h1>Score: <span class="score"></span></h1>
            <p>
                You got <span class="correct"></span>
                out of <span class="count"></span> notes correct.
            </p>
            <p>
                Note accuracy: <span class="note-accuracy"></span>%<br/>
                Timing accuracy: <span class="timing-accuracy"></span>%
            </p>
        </div>
```

The `<div id="results-panel">` element will be shown when the game is completed. We add the `<span>` placeholders to show a score, the total number of notes along with the number of correct ones, and some accuracy statistics.

```
<div class="keyboard">
    <div class="keys">
        <!-- Code not shown... -->
    </div>
    <div class="controls">
        <button id="stop-button">Stop</button>
        <button id="restart-button">Restart</button>
        <button id="quit-button">Quit</button><br/>
        <label for="sustain">Sustain: </label>
        <input type="checkbox" id="sustain" checked /><br />
        <label for="volume">Volume: </label>
        <input type="range" id="volume" min="1" max="100"
            value="100" step="1" />
    </div>
</div>
</div>
```

We also added some buttons to the `<div class="controls">` element below the keyboard. The **Stop** button will stop the game, **Restart** will start the current song over from the beginning, and **Quit** will take the player back to the splash panel.

Now let's create a `GamePanel` object in a file named `gamePanel.js` to contain all of the code needed to implement the game. The constructor will take a reference to the `audioManager` object:

```
function GamePanel(audioManager)
{
    var $panel = $("#game"),
        $notesPanel = $("#notes-panel"),
        $resultsPanel = $("#results-panel"),
        practiceMode = false,
        noteCount = 0,
        notesCorrect = 0,
        score = 0,
        keyCodesToNotes = {},
        sustain = true,
        volume = 1.0;
```

Here we define a few variables to keep track of the game state. The `practiceMode` variable determines if we are playing the game or practicing. `noteCount`, `notesCorrect` and `score` are used to keep track of how the player is doing.

We move all of the code to support the keyboard from the `PianoHeroApp` object to the `GamePanel` object. This includes the `keyCodesToNotes`, `sustain`, and `volume` variables. We also move the `initKeyboard()`, `keyDown()`, `keyUp()`, `pressPianoKey()`, `releasePianoKey()`, `getPianoKeyElement()`, and `isInputTypeSupported()` methods. Finally, we move the `onKeyDown()` and `onKeyUp()` event handlers.

Now let's add some public methods for the application to interact with the game panel. Like the splash panel, we need methods to show and hide it:

```
this.show = function()
{
    $panel.fadeIn(startGame);
    return this;
};
this.hide = function()
{
    $panel.hide();
    return this;
};
```

The `show()` public method fades the game panel in. We pass in a reference to the `startGame()` method, which we will write in the next section, to be called when the fade in has completed.

What just happened?

We created the game panel by adding markup for an area to hold animated `note` elements, and an area to show the score. These are in addition to our keyboard we created in the previous chapter. Then, we created a JavaScript object to hold all of the code for the game panel, including all of the code we wrote previously for the keyboard.

Time for action – creating the controller

At this point there's not much left in our main application object, `PianoHeroApp`. We moved all of the code to load the audio to the `SplashPanel` object, and all of the code to make the keyboard work to the `GamePanel` object.

The `PianoHeroApp` object will now only act as a state controller to hide and show the correct panels. First we need to add some variables to hold references to the panels:

```
function PianoHeroApp()
{
    var version = "7.1",
        audioManager = new AudioManager("audio"),
        splashPanel = new SplashPanel(audioManager),
```

```
        gamePanel = new GamePanel(audioManager),
        curPanel = undefined;
```

We define variables to hold the audio manager, the splash panel, and the game panel objects. We also have a `curPanel` variable, which will be set to the current panel that is showing. To start with we will set it to `undefined`.

Next, we will create a private `showPanel()` method that will hide the currently showing panel, if there is one, and show a different one:

```
function showPanel(panel)
{
    if (curPanel) curPanel.hide();
    curPanel = panel;
    curPanel.show();
}
```

This method takes the panel to show as a parameter. This will be a reference to either `SplashPanel` or `GamePanel`. First we check to see if a panel is showing, and if so we call its `hide()` method. Then we set `curPanel` to the new panel and call its `show()` method.

Next we define the public `startGame()` method. If you remember from the code we wrote for the `SplashPanel` object, this will get called from the event handler when the user clicks either on the **Play Game** or **Play Song** button. It passes in the game options the player selected:

```
this.startGame = function(songName, rate, playGame)
{
    gamePanel.setOptions(songName, rate, playGame);
    showPanel(gamePanel);
};
```

The `startGame()` method takes three parameters; the name of the song to play, the playback rate (which controls how fast the game progresses), and a Boolean value (which determines if the user clicked on the **Play Game** button).

First we call the `setOptions()` method of the `GamePanel` object, which we will write later. We pass through the same parameters we got from the splash panel. Then we call the `showPanel()` method passing in the `GamePanel` object. This is what will start the game.

Next we will define the public `quitGame()` method. This will be called from the game panel when the user clicks on the **Quit** button:

```
this.quitGame = function()
{
    showPanel(splashPanel);
};
```

All we do in this method is call `showPanel()`, passing it the `SplashPanel` object.

The final thing we need to define is the `start()` method of our application:

```
this.start = function()
{
    $(document).keydown(function(e) { curPanel.onKeyDown(e); })
               .keyup(function(e) { curPanel.onKeyUp(e); });

    showPanel(splashPanel);
    splashPanel.loadAudio();
};
```

First we set up keyboard event handlers on the document, just as we did when creating the piano application. However, in this application we will forward the keyboard event to the current panel. By centralizing the keyboard event handlers in the application object, we don't have to write a bunch of code in each panel to subscribe and unsubscribe keyboard event handlers from the document when the panel is shown or hidden.

The final thing we do is show the splash panel, and then call its `loadAudio()` method to kickstart the application.

> Our splash and game panels implement `show()`, `hide()`, `keydown()`, and `keyup()` methods. Since JavaScript is untyped we can't enforce this with interfaces. So we program by convention instead, assuming that all panels will implement those methods.

What just happened?

We added code to the main application object to control the state of the game. When the player clicks on one of the buttons from the splash panel it starts the game, and when they click on **Quit** from the game, it shows the splash panel.

Creating an audio sequencer

Before we can play the game, we need some way to play songs on the piano by playing back notes in a certain order, at the correct time, and at the correct speed. We will create an object called `AudioSequencer` that takes an array of musical event objects and turns them into music.

To implement our audio sequencer we need to define a format for our music events. We will roughly follow the MIDI format, but much more simplified. MIDI is the standard to record and play back music events. Each event contains information about how and when to play notes, or turn notes off.

Our event object will contain three fields:

- `deltaTime`: The amount of time to wait before executing the event.
- `event`: This is an integer event code that determines what the event does. It can be one of the following:
  - Turn a note on
  - Turn a note off
  - Cue point will be at the beginning of a song
  - End of track will signal that the song is over
- `note`: This is the note to play. It contains the octave and note, and matches our audio file names, for example, 3C.

The audio sequencer will work by looking at the `deltaTime` field in each event to determine how long to wait before firing the event. The client will pass in an event handler function that will be called when the event is fired. The client will then look at the event data and determine which note to play. This loop continues until there are no more events left.

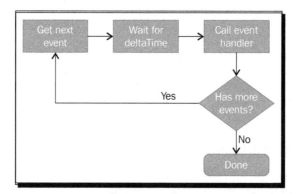

Time for action – creating AudioSequencer

Let's create our `AudioSequencer` object in a file called `audioSequencer.js`. We'll start by defining a few variables:

```
function AudioSequencer()
{
    var _events = [],
        _playbackRate = 1,
        _playing = false,
        eventHandler = undefined,
        timeoutID = 0;
```

First we define an `_events` array to hold all of the music events to play. The `_playbackRate` variable controls how fast the song plays. A value of 1 will be at normal speed, less than 1 slower, and more than 1 faster. The `_playing` variable is set to `true` while a song is playing. `eventHandler` will be set to a function that gets called when an event is fired, and `timeoutID` will contain the handle returned from `setTimeout()` in case the user stops the game and we need to cancel the timeout.

Now let's define some public property methods. The first is `events()`. It is used to get or set the `_events` array:

```
this.events = function(newEvents)
{
    if (newEvents) {
        _events = newEvents;
        return this;
    }
    return _events;
};
```

The next is `playbackRate()`. It is used to get or set `_playbackRate`:

```
this.playbackRate = function(newRate)
{
    if (newRate) {
        _playbackRate = newRate;
        return this;
    }
    return _playbackRate;
};
```

Finally we have `isPlaying()`, which is used to determine if a song is currently playing:

```
this.isPlaying = function()
{
    return _playing;
};
```

Now we will code the public `startPlayback()` method. This method takes two parameters; the event handler function and optionally the starting position, which is an index into the `_events` array:

```
this.startPlayback = function(callback, startPos)
{
    startPos = startPos || 0;

    if (!_playing && _events.length > 0)
```

```
        {
            _playing = true;
            eventHandler = callback;
            playEvent(startPos);
            return true;
        }
        return false;
    };
```

The first thing we do is default the `startPos` parameter to `0`, if it was not provided. Next we check that a song isn't already playing, and make sure we actually have some events to play. If so we set the `_playing` flag to `true`, store the event handler reference, and then call `playEvent()` for the first event. We return `true` if playback was successfully started.

Now let's write the `playEvent()` method. It takes one parameter, the index of the next event to fire:

```
        function playEvent(index)
        {
            var event = _events[index];
            eventHandler(event.event, event.note, index);

            index++;
            if (index < _events.length)
            {
                timeoutID = setTimeout(function()
                {
                    playEvent(index);
                },
                _events[index].deltaTime * (1 / _playbackRate));
            }
            else _playing = false; // all done
        }
```

The first thing we do is get the event at the specified index in the `_events` array. Then we immediately call the event handler's callback function that was provided in the `startPlayback()` method, passing it the event code, the note to play, and the event index.

Next we increment the index to get the next event. If there is another event we call `setTimeout()` to wait for the amount of time specified in the event's `deltaTime` field before calling `playEvent()`, again passing it the index of the next event. We compute the amount of time to wait by multiplying `deltaTime` by the inverse of the playback rate. For example, if the playback rate is 0.5 then the wait time will be 1 , 0.5 or 2 times the normal rate. This loop continues in this fashion until there are no more events to play.

The last thing we need is a public `stopPlayback()` method. This method is called to stop the event loop, and therefore stop the playback of the audio events:

```
this.stopPlayback = function()
{
    if (_playing)
    {
        _playing = false;
        if (timeoutID) clearTimeout(timeoutID);
        eventHandler = undefined;
    }
};
```

First we check the `_playing` flag to make sure a song is actually playing. If so, we set the flag to `false`, and then we call `clearTimeout()` to stop the timeout. This will stop `playEvent()` from being called again, which will stop the playback loop.

The last thing we need is to define the playback event codes, so we don't have to remember the event code numbers. We will define a pseudo enumeration using an object on `AudioSequencer` called `eventCodes`:

```
AudioSequencer.eventCodes =
{
    noteOn: 1,
    noteOff: 2,
    cuePoint: 3,
    endOfTrack: 4
};
```

What just happened?

We created an audio sequencer object that takes an array of music events, similar to MIDI events, and calls them at the correct time using the `setTimeout()` function. When an event is fired it calls the event handler function, passed in by the game panel.

 Although we have written this code to play music, you could use the same technique anywhere you need things to happen at predetermined intervals.

Playing a song

Now that we have an audio sequencer, we can go into the game panel and add some code to play a song in practice mode. As the song plays it will press the correct keys on the screen, just like a player piano. Later we will add code to check for player interaction to see how good they follow along with the song.

Time for action – adding the audio sequencer

Let's add the audio sequencer to the game panel. We will go into the GamePanel object and add an instance of AudioSequencer to it:

```
function GamePanel(audioManager)
{
    var sequencer = new AudioSequencer();
```

Next let's write the public setOptions() method, which is called from the startGame() method of PianoHeroApp. It takes three parameters; the song name, playback rate, and whether to play the game or the song in practice mode:

```
this.setOptions = function(songName, rate, playGame)
{
    sequencer.events(musicData[songName])
            .playbackRate(rate);
    practiceMode = !playGame;
    return this;
};
```

The first thing we do is set the events() property of the audio sequencer to the data for the song to play. We get the song data from the musicData object, which is defined in musicData.js. Then, we set the audio sequencer's playbackRate() property. Lastly we set the practiceMode variable.

The musicData object contains event data that the sequencer can play for all of the songs that the user can select on the splash page. Each song is defined as an array of music event objects. Here's an example of what the data looks like for the rhyme *Twinkle, Twinkle Little Star*:

```
var musicData =
{
    littleStar: [
        { deltaTime: 0, event: 3, note: null },
        { deltaTime: 0, event: 1, note: "3C" },
        { deltaTime: 500, event: 2, note: "3C" },
        { deltaTime: 0, event: 1, note: "3C" },
```

```
            { deltaTime: 500, event: 2, note: "3C" },
            { deltaTime: 0, event: 1, note: "3G" },
            { deltaTime: 500, event: 2, note: "3G" },
            // ...
            { deltaTime: 0, event: 4, note: null }
        ]
    };
```

It starts with a cue point event (event: 3), and then turns on note 3C (event: 1). After 500 milliseconds it turns off note 3C (event: 2). It continues on until the last event, which is end of track (event: 4).

Next let's write the startGame() method, which is called from the show() method:

```
function startGame()
{
    $resultsPanel.hide();
    $notesPanel.show();
    // Reset score
    noteCount = 0;
    notesCorrect = 0;
    score = 0;
    // Start interval for notes animation
    intervalId = setInterval(function() { updateNotes(); },
        1000 / framesPerSecond);
    // Start playback of the song
    sequencer.startPlayback(onAudioEvent, 0);
}
```

The first thing we do is hide the results panel and show the notes panel. Then we reset the score and statistics.

Next, we start an interval timer by calling the JavaScript setInterval() function and setting the intervalId variable to the handle that is returned. We will use that later to stop the interval when the game has finished, or the player stops the game. This interval is used to animate the elements in the notes panel that fall down from the top of the page. We set the interval to fire at a constant rate by dividing 1000 milliseconds by the number of frames per second. We will use a frame rate of 30 frames per second, which is enough to produce a relatively smooth animation and not bog down the game. At every interval of the timer we call the updateNotes() method, which we'll write in the next section.

The final thing we do in this method is call the `startPlayback()` method of the audio sequencer, passing it a reference to our audio event handler method, `onAudioEvent()`, and a start position of zero:

```
function onAudioEvent(eventCode, note)
{
    switch (eventCode)
    {
        case AudioSequencer.eventCodes.noteOn:
            addNote(note);
            break;
        case AudioSequencer.eventCodes.endOfTrack:
            sequencer.stopPlayback();
            break;
    }
}
```

This method accepts two parameters: the audio event code and the note to play. We use a `switch` statement along with our `eventCodes` enumeration to determine how to handle the event. If the event code is `noteOn`, we call the `addNote()` method to add a `note` element to the notes panel. If it's an `endOfTrack` event, we call `stopPlayback()` on the audio sequencer. We can ignore all of the other events for now.

What just happened?

We added the audio sequencer to our game panel and hooked up a function to handle when note events are fired. We added a `startGame()` method that starts the animation interval for animating the `note` elements.

Creating animated notes

Now we are going to implement the code for the notes panel. This is where the animation of notes dropping from the top of the page happens. It works something like this:

- The audio sequencer sends an event that a note should be played (see `onAudioEvent()` in the previous section).

- The note is not actually played at that time. Instead a rectangular element that represents the note is added to the top of the notes panel.

- Every time our animation interval timer fires, the y-position of the `note` element is incremented so that it moves down.

- When the element hits the bottom edge of the notes panel (and the top edge of the keyboard), it plays the audio clip associated with the note.
- When the element completely leaves the notes panel, it is removed from the DOM.

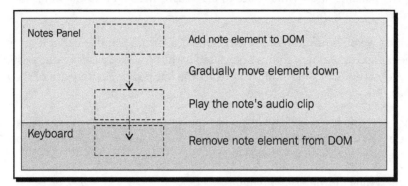

Time for action – adding notes

Let's write the `addNote()` method that was referenced by `onAudioEvent()` in the previous section. This method takes one parameter, the name of the note to add:

```
function addNote(note)
{
    noteCount++;
    // Add a new note element
    var $note = $("<div class='note'></div>");
    $note.data("note", note);
    $notesPanel.append($note);

    var $key = getPianoKeyElement(note);
    // Position the note element over the piano key
    $note.css("top", "0")
        .css("left", $key.position().left)
        .css("width", $key.css("width"));

    if ($key.hasClass("black"))
    {
        $note.addClass("black");
    }
}
```

First we update the `noteCount` variable to keep track of statistics. Then we create a new note `<div>` element using jQuery, and give it a class of `"note"`. We set the `data-note` custom attribute to the name of the note. We will need that later when it reaches the bottom of the panel to know which note to play. Lastly, we add it to the notes panel using jQuery's `append()` method.

The next thing we do is position the `note` element over the piano key that it represents. We get the piano key element that is associated with the note by calling our existing `getPianoKeyElement()` method. We extract the left position and width of the piano key, and set the `note` element to the same values so that it lines up.

The final thing we do is check if the piano key is a black or white key, by checking if it has the `"black"` class defined on it. If so, we give the `note` element a `"black"` class too. This will make the element appear in a different color.

Let's add the styling for the `note` elements:

```
#notes-panel .note
{
    position: absolute;
    display: block;
    width: 50px;
    height: 20px;
    background-color: cyan;
    /* browser specific gradients not shown */
    background: linear-gradient(left, white, cyan);
    box-shadow: 0 0 4px 4px rgba(255, 255, 255, 0.7);
}
```

We set the `position` to `absolute` because we need to move them around and place them wherever we want. We give them a linear gradient from left to right, fading from white to cyan. We also give it a white shadow with no offset. This will make it look like it's glowing against the black background:

```
#notes-panel .note.black
{
    background-color: magenta;
    /* browser specific gradients not shown */
    background: linear-gradient(left, white, magenta);
}
```

The notes with the `"black"` class will override the background color to fade from white to magenta.

What just happened?

We created a method that adds elements that represent notes to the notes panel. We positioned those notes so that they are directly over the top of the piano key they belong to.

Time for action – animating the notes

Previously, we started an interval using `setInterval()` in the `startGame()` method. The `updateNotes()` method gets called every time the interval expires. This method is responsible for updating the position of all of the `note` elements, so they appear to move down the screen:

```
function updateNotes()
{
    $(".note", $notesPanel).each(function()
    {
        var $note = $(this);
        var top = $note.position().top;
        if (top <= 200)
        {
            // Move the note down
            top += pixelsPerFrame;
            $note.css("top", top);
            if (top + 20 > 200)
            {
                // The note hit the bottom of the panel
                currentNote.note = $note.data("note");
                currentNote.time = getCurrentTime();
                currentNote.$note = $note;
                if (practiceMode) pressPianoKey($note.data("note"));
            }
        }
        else
        {
            // Note is below the panel, remove it
            if (practiceMode) releasePianoKey($note.data("note"));
            $note.remove();
        }
    });

    // Check if there are any notes left
    if ($(".note", $notesPanel).length == 0)
    {
        // No more notes, game over man
```

```
            if (!practiceMode) showScore();
            endGame();
        }
    }
```

First we select all of the note elements in the notes panel and iterate over them.
For each one we do the following:

- Get the top position and check if it is less than 200, which is the height of the notes panel.

- If the element is still inside the notes panel, we move the element down the number of pixels defined by the pixelsPerFrame variable. At 30 frames per second this is 2 pixels.

- Next we check if the bottom of the note element hit the bottom of the notes panel by checking if the bottom is more than 200.

- If so, we set the currentNote object's note variable to the note, so we can check if the user played the correct note later. We also get the exact time the note hit the bottom, to determine how close the player was to playing it on time.

- If we are in practice mode, we also play the note by calling pressPianoKey() and passing it the note element.

- If the note element is outside of the notes panel, then we call releasePianoKey() and remove it from the DOM.

The final thing we do is check if there are any more note elements left in the notes panel. If not, the game is over and we call showScore() to show the results panel. Then we call endGame(), which stops the animation interval.

What just happened?

We animated the note elements so that they appear to fall down the screen over the keys of the keyboard that they represent. When the notes hit the bottom of the notes panel, we play the note if in practice mode. When the note element moves out of the panel, we remove it from the DOM.

Have a go hero

Try playing around with the frame rate and see how it affects the quality of the animation. What is the lowest frame rate that is acceptable? What is the highest frame rate that is perceptible?

Handling user input

The user has started the game and notes are falling down the screen. Now we need to check if the player presses the correct piano key at the correct time. When they do, we will give them some points based on how accurate they were.

Time for action – checking the notes

We will add a call to the `checkNote()` method in the `keyDown()` method. The `checkNote()` method takes the name of the note as a parameter, and checks if there is a `note` element at the bottom of the notes panel that matches it:

```
function checkNote(note)
{
    if (currentNote.note == note)
    {
        var dif = getCurrentTime() - currentNote.time;
        if (dif < gracePeriod)
        {
            notesCorrect++;
            score += Math.round(10 * (gracePeriod - dif) /
                gracePeriod);
            currentNote.$note.css("background", "green");
            addHitEffect();
        }
    }
}
```

First we check the `currentNote` object that was set previously in `updateNotes()`. If its note is the same as the one the user played, then they might get some points for playing it at the correct time. To find out if they get points, we first find the time difference in milliseconds between the time the note hit the bottom of the panel and the current time. If it's within the allowable grace period, which we set to 200 milliseconds, then we compute the score.

We first increment the number of correct notes. Then, we determine the score by computing the percentage of time they were off by and multiplying it by 10. This way the number of points per note is between 1 and 10. Finally, to give the user some indication that they got it right, we change the background color of the element to green and call `addHitEffect()`:

```
function addHitEffect()
{
    var $title = $(".title", $notesPanel);
    $title.css("color", "#012");
    setTimeout(function() { $title.css("color", "black"); }, 100);
}
```

The `addHitEffect()` method flashes the **PIANO HERO** title in the background of the notes panel by changing its color, waiting for 100 milliseconds using a `setTimeout()` call, and then changing it back to black.

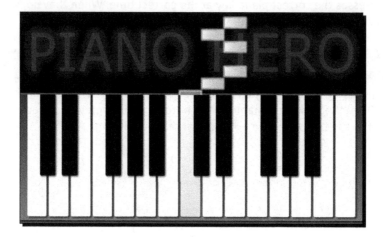

What just happened?

We added a method to check if the correct piano key was pressed at the correct time for a `note` element. If so, we add points depending on how well timed the note was played, and change the color of the note to indicate success.

Ending the game

Now the player can play the game and we can keep track of the score and the number of notes they got correct. When the game ends, we need to display the results panel that shows the score and some statistics.

Time for action – creating the results panel

After all of the notes have been played for the song, the `updateNotes()` method calls `showScore()`, where we will show the player's score and some statistics:

```
function showScore()
{
    $notesPanel.hide();
    $resultsPanel.fadeIn();
    $(".score", $resultsPanel).text(score);
    $(".correct", $resultsPanel).text(notesCorrect);
    $(".count", $resultsPanel).text(noteCount);
    $(".note-accuracy", $resultsPanel).text(
```

```
        Math.round(100 * notesCorrect / noteCount));
    $(".timing-accuracy", $resultsPanel).text(
        Math.round(10 * score / notesCorrect));
}
```

First we hide the notes panel and fade in the score panel in its place. Then, we fill in the score and statistics into the placeholders in the DOM. We show the score, number of notes correct, and total number of notes. In addition, we compute the percentage of notes they got correct using the `notesCorrect` and `noteCount` variables.

We get the timing accuracy percentage by factoring it from the score and number of notes correct. Remember that there are a total of 10 points possible per note, so if they got 17 notes correct the total number of possible points is 170. If the score was 154 that would be 154 / 170 ≈ 91%.

What just happened?

We showed the results panel when the game is over, and populated it with the player's score and statistics. Our game is now finished. Go ahead and give it a try and become a piano hero!

Have a go hero

Try writing an audio recorder class that records when the user plays a note on the keyboard, and saves it to an array of data objects that can be played by the audio sequencer.

Pop quiz

Q1. Which JavaScript function can be used to create a timer that fires at regular intervals until cleared?

1. `setTimeout()`
2. `setRate()`
3. `setInterval()`
4. `wait()`

Q2. Which attributes of a `<progress>` element control the percentage of the progress bar that is marked complete?

1. `value` **and** `max`
2. `currentValue` **and** `maxValue`
3. `start` **and** `end`
4. `min` **and** `max`

Summary

We created a game based on the piano application we wrote in the previous chapter. We used JavaScript timers to implement an audio sequencer to play back songs and create an animation loop. We created splash and game panels and learned how to transition game states between them.

We covered the following concepts in this chapter:

◆ How to create a splash panel and use text shadows to produce interesting text effects

◆ How to use an HTML5 progress bar element to show the progress of loading dynamic resources

◆ Using JavaScript timer functions to create an audio sequencer, to control playback of audio to play songs

◆ How to animate DOM elements using a JavaScript timer

◆ How to transition between game states and panels

◆ How to collect user input, verify it, and show the results at the end of the game

In the next chapter, we will learn all about using Ajax to dynamically load resources and call web services by building a weather widget.

8
A Change in the Weather

"Climate is what we expect, weather is what we get."

– Mark Twain

In this chapter, we will build a weather widget to learn about using Ajax to load content asynchronously and communicate with web services. We will learn about Ajax and how to use jQuery's Ajax methods to load files that contain XML or JSON formatted data. Then we will get the weather conditions from a web service to display in the widget. We will also use the HTML Geolocation API to find the user's location so we can show their local weather.

We will learn the following in this chapter:

◆ How to get XML and JSON data using jQuery' Ajax methods

◆ Parsing JSON versus XML returned from services

◆ What web services are and how to communicate with them asynchronously using Ajax

◆ The problem with cross site scripting, and the solution JSONP

◆ How to use HTML5 Geolocation API to get the user's location

◆ How to connect to a web service to get the current weather report

Introduction to Ajax

Ajax is a technology used by JavaScript to send data to, and receive data from, a server. Originally **Ajax** stood for **Asynchronous JavaScript and XML**, but now this meaning has been lost as JSON (which we learned about in *Chapter 1, The Task at Hand*) has begun to replace XML as the preferred format for packaging data, and Ajax requests do not need to be asynchronous.

Using Ajax will make your applications more dynamic and responsive. Rather than having postbacks whenever you need to update a part of a web page, you can load only the necessary data and update the page dynamically. With Ajax we can retrieve almost anything from the server, including HTML snippets to be inserted into the web page and static data to be used by the application. We can also call web services that provide access to things such as data and services that are only available on the server side.

Making Ajax requests

jQuery provides methods that make it easy to access web resources and call web services using Ajax. The `ajax()` method is the most primitive of them. If you want to have the most control over service calls you can use this method. Most of the time it is preferable to use one of the higher level methods such as `get()` or `post()`.

The `get()` method makes it easier to do an HTTP GET request using Ajax. At its simplest, you pass in the URL of the resource or service you want to get and it asynchronously sends the request and gets the response. When it's done it executes a callback function that you provide.

For example, the following code snippet makes a GET request for an XML file on the server, and displays its contents in a dialog:

```
$.get("data/myData.xml", function(data) {
    alert("data: " + data);
});
```

All of the jQuery Ajax methods return an object that you can attach `done()`, `fail()`, and `always()` callback methods to. The `done()` method gets called after the request is successful, `fail()` gets called if there was an error, and `always()` gets called last whether the request succeeded or failed:

```
$.get("data/myData.xml")
    .done(function(data) { alert("data: " + data); })
    .fail(function() { alert("error"); })
    .always(function() { alert("done"); });
```

The data that gets passed to the `done()` method will be either an XML root element, a JSON object, or a string depending on the MIME type specified in the response. If it's a JSON object, you can reference the data as you would any JavaScript object. If it's an XML element you can use jQuery to traverse the data.

You may provide query parameters to the request by passing in an object literal of name/value pairs:

```
$.get("services/getInfo.php", {
    firstName: "John",
    lastName: "Doe"
})
.done(function(data) { /* do something */ });
```

This will make the following request:

```
services/getInfo.php?firstName=John&lastName=Doe
```

Use the `post()` method if you prefer to make a POST request rather than GET, which may be preferable if you are using a secure protocol such as HTTPS, and don't want the query parameters visible on the request:

```
$.post("services/getInfo.php", {
    firstName: "John",
    lastName: "Doe"
});
```

 In some browsers, including Chrome, you can't access files with Ajax requests using the `file://` protocol. In that case you will need to run your application through a web server such as IIS or Apache, or use a different browser.

Time for action – creating a weather widget

Throughout this chapter we will demonstrate how to make various Ajax calls by implementing a widget that shows a weather report. Let's start by defining the widget's HTML markup:

```
<div id="weather-widget">
  <div class="loading">
    <p>Checking the weather...</p>
    <img src="images/loading.gif" alt="Loading..."/>
  </div>
  <div class="results">
    <header>
```

```
        <img src="" alt="Condition"/>Current weather for
        <div class="location"><span></span></div>
     </header>
     <section class="conditions">
        Conditions: <span data-field="weather"></span><br/>
        Temperature: <span data-field="temperature_string"></span><br/>
        Feels Like: <span data-field="feelslike_string"></span><br/>
        Humidity: <span data-field="relative_humidity"></span><br/>
        Wind: <span data-field="wind_string"></span><br/>
     </section>
   </div>
   <div class="error">
     Error: <span></span>
   </div>
</div>
```

The widget consists of three different panels, only one of which will show at any given time. The `<div class="loading">` panel will be visible while the weather data is being retrieved from the server. It has an animated image in it to indicate to the user that something is loading.

The `<div class="results">` panel will show the weather data that was returned from the server. It contains placeholder fields for us to put the weather data into. Notice that we are using custom data attributes on the placeholder `<span>` elements. Those will be used later to extract the correct data from the XML document or JSON object returned by the server.

The `<div class="error">` panel will show an error message if the Ajax request failed.

Now let's create the JavaScript code to control the widget in a new file named `weatherWidget.js`. We will create a `WeatherWidget` object whose constructor takes a reference to the widget's root element wrapped in a jQuery object:

```
function WeatherWidget($widget)
{
    this.update = function()
    {
        $(".results", $widget).hide();
        $(".loading", $widget).show();
        getWeatherReport();
    };

    function getWeatherReport() {
        // not implemented
    }
}
```

In our object we create one public method called `update()`. This will be called from the page to tell the widget to update the weather report. In the `update()` method we first hide the results panel and show the loading panel. Then we call the `getWeatherReport()` method, which will make the Ajax call and update the widget when it is finished. We will write different versions of this method in the next few sections.

What just happened?

We created a weather widget that can be placed on any page in a website. It has a public `update()` method that is called to tell the widget to update its information.

Time for action – getting XML data

First let's create an example of getting data from an XML file and updating the weather widget from its data. We will create a new web page called `weather.html` and put the markup for the weather widget into it. This page will have a **Check Weather** button. When clicked, it will call the weather widget's `update()` method. You can find the code for this example in `Chapter 8/example8.1`.

Next we need to create an XML file with some weather information in it. We will name the file `weather.xml` and place it in the `data` folder:

```
<weather>
    <location>Your City</location>
    <current_observation>
        <weather>Snow</weather>
        <temperature_string>38.3 F (3.5 C)</temperature_string>
        <feelslike_string>38 F (3 C)</feelslike_string>
        <relative_humidity>76%</relative_humidity>
        <wind_string>From the WSW at 1.0 MPH</wind_string>
        <icon_url>images/snow.gif</icon_url>
    </current_observation>
</weather>
```

Now let's write the `getWeatherReport()` method in the `WeatherWidget` object:

```
function getWeatherReport()
{
    $.get("data/weather.xml")
        .done(function(data) {
            populateWeather(data);
        })
        .fail(function(jqXHR, textStatus, errorThrown) {
            showError(errorThrown);
        });
}
```

In this method we use the jQuery `get()` method to perform the Ajax request and pass it the path to our XML file. If the server call is successful we call the `populateWeather()` method, passing it the data returned from the request. This will be the root element of a DOM that represents our XML file. If the request fails we call the `showError()` method, passing it the error message.

Next let's write the `populateWeather()` method. This is where we will extract the data from the XML document and insert it into the page:

```
function populateWeather(data)
{
    var $observation = $("current_observation", data);

    $(".results header img", $widget)
        .attr("src", $("icon_url", $observation).text());
    $(".location>span", $widget)
        .text($("location", data).text());

    $(".conditions>span").each(function(i, e)
    {
        var $span = $(this);
        var field = $span.data("field");
        $(this).text($(field, $observation).text());
    });

    $(".loading", $widget).fadeOut(function ()
    {
        $(".results", $widget).fadeIn();
    });
}
```

We need a way to extract data from the XML document retrieved from the server. Fortunately for us, jQuery can be used to select elements from any XML document, not just the web page's DOM. All we have to do is pass in the root element or our XML as the second parameter to a jQuery select. This is exactly what we do in the first line of the method to get the `current_observation` element and store it in the `$observation` variable.

Next we use jQuery to get the text from the `icon_url` element, and set the image's `src` attribute to it. This is an image that represents the current weather. We also get the text from the `location element` and insert that into the widget's header.

Then we iterate over all of the `<span>` elements in the conditions section of the widget. For each one we get the value of its `data-field` custom data attribute. We use that to find the element with the same name inside the `current_observation` element, get its text, and put it into the `<span>` element.

The last thing we do is fade out the loading panel and fade in the results panel, to show the current weather on the page. Here's what it looks like with the data loaded:

What just happened?

We loaded an XML file from the server that contains weather data using jQuery's `get()` Ajax method. Then, we extracted the information from the XML document using jQuery selects and put it into the widget's placeholder elements to show it on the page.

Time for action – getting JSON data

Now let's do the same thing as we did in the previous section, except that we will get the data from a file containing JSON formatted data rather than XML. The concept is the same, except that what we get back from the Ajax call is a JavaScript object rather than an XML document. You can find the code for this example in `Chapter 8/example8.2`.

First let's define our JSON file, which we will name `weather.json`, and put it in the `data` folder:

```
{
    "location": {
        "city":"Your City"
    }
    ,"current_observation": {
        "weather":"Clear",
        "temperature_string":"38.3 F (3.5 C)",
        "wind_string":"From the WSW at 1.0 MPH Gusting to 5.0 MPH",
        "feelslike_string":"38 F (3 C)",
        "relative_humidity":"71%",
        "icon_url":"images/nt_clear.gif"
    }
}
```

This JSON defines an anonymous wrapping object with a `location` object and a `current_observation` object inside of it. The `current_observation` object contains all of the data that the `current_observation` element had in the XML document.

Now let's rewrite `getWeatherReport()` to get the JSON data:

```
function getWeatherReport()
{
    $.get("data/weather.json", {
        t: new Date().getTime()
    })
    .done(function(data) { populateWeather(data); })
    .fail(function(jqXHR, textStatus, errorThrown) {
        showError(errorThrown);
    });
}
```

We still use the `get()` method, but now we are getting the JSON file. Notice how this time we are adding a query parameter to the URL set to the current time in milliseconds. This is a way to get around the browser's caching. Most browsers don't seem to recognize when files have changed using Ajax requests. By adding a parameter that changes every time we make the request, it fools the browser into thinking it's a new request, bypassing the cached one. The request will look something like `data/weather.json?t=1365127077960`.

> When running this application through a web server such as IIS, you may need to add the `.json` file type to the list of MIME types for your site (`.json`, `application/json`). Otherwise you will get an error that the file is not found.

Now let's rewrite the `populateWeather()` method:

```
function populateWeather(data)
{
    var observation = data.current_observation;

    $(".results header img", $widget).attr("src",
        observation.icon_url);
    $(".location>span", $widget).text(data.location.city);

    $(".conditions>span").each(function(i, e)
    {
        var $span = $(this);
        var field = $span.data("field");
        $(this).text(observation[field]);
    });
```

```
    $(".loading", $widget).fadeOut(function ()
    {
        $(".results", $widget).fadeIn();
    });
}
```

This time jQuery recognizes that we have loaded data in JSON format, and automatically converts it to a JavaScript object. So that's what gets passed into the method's data parameter. To get the observation data we can now simply access the current_observation field of the data object.

Just like before, we iterate over all of the <span> placeholder elements, but this time we use square brackets to access the data from the observation object using the field custom data attribute as the field name.

What just happened?

We rewrote the weather widget to get the weather data from a JSON formatted file. Since jQuery automatically converts JSON data into JavaScript objects, we were able to directly access the data rather than use jQuery to search through an XML document.

HTML5 Geolocation API

Later we will rewrite the weather widget once again to get the weather from a web service instead of a static file on the server. We want to show the user the weather for their current location, so we need some way to determine where the user is. HTML5 has just the thing for that: the Geolocation API.

Geolocation is widely supported by nearly every modern browser. The accuracy of the location depends on the capabilities of the user's device. Devices that have GPS will give you a very accurate location, while those that don't will try to determine the user's location as close as they can by some other means, such as by IP address.

The Geolocation API is accessed by using the navigator.geolocation object. To get the user's location you call the getCurrentPosition() method. It takes two parameters- a callback function if it succeeds and a callback function if it fails:

```
navigator.geolocation.getCurrentPosition(
    function(position) { alert("call was successful"); },
    function(error) { alert("call failed"); }
);
```

The function that is called on success gets an object passed into it that contains another object named `coords`. The following is a list of some of the more useful fields the `coords` object contains:

- `latitude`: This is the user's latitude in decimal degrees (for example, 44.6770429).
- `longitude`: This is the user's longitude in decimal degrees (for example, -85.60261659).
- `accuracy`: This is the accuracy of the position in meters.
- `speed`: This is the speed the user is moving in meters per second. This is available for devices with GPS.
- `heading`: This is the heading degrees that the user is moving in. Like speed this is for devices with GPS.

For example, if you wanted to get the user's location you would do the following:

```
var loc = position.coords.latitude + ", " +
position.coords.longitude);
```

The user must allow your page to use the Geolocation API. If they reject your request, the call to `getCurrentPosition()` will fail, and depending on the browser your error handler may get called or fail silently. This is what the request looks like in Chrome:

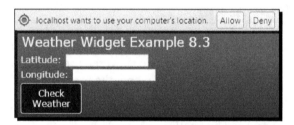

The error handler gets passed an error object that contains two fields, `code` and `message`. The `code` field is an integer error code and `message` is the error message string. There are three possible error codes: `permission denied`, `position unavailable`, or `timeout`.

The Geolocation API also has a `watchPosition()` method. It works the same as `getCurrentPosition()`, except that your callback function gets called whenever the user moves. This way you can track the user and update their position in your application in real time.

 In some browsers you must be running the web page through a web server such as IIS or Apache for geolocation to work.

Time for action – getting geolocation data

In this section we will add some code to our weather widget example to access the Geolocation API. You can find the code for this section in chapter8/example8.3.

First let's go into weather.html and add a section to show the user's location next to the **Check Weather** button:

```
<div id="controls">
    <div>
        Latitude: <input id="latitude" type="text"/><br/>
        Longitude: <input id="longitude" type="text"/>
    </div>
    <button id="getWeather">Check Weather</button>
    <div class="error">
        Error: <span></span>
    </div>
</div>
```

We add a `<div>` element with text fields to show the user's latitude and longitude that we got from the Geolocation API. We also add a `<div class="error">` element to show the error message if geolocation fails.

Now let's go into weather.js and add some code to the WeatherApp object. We will add a getLocation() method:

```
function getLocation()
{
    if (navigator.geolocation)
    {
        navigator.geolocation.getCurrentPosition(
        function(position)
        {
            $("#latitude").val(position.coords.latitude);
            $("#longitude").val(position.coords.longitude);
        },
        function(error)
        {
            $("#controls .error")
                .text("ERROR: " + error.message)
                .slideDown();
        });
    }
}
```

First we check that the Geolocation API is available by checking that the geolocation object exists in the navigation object. Then we call geolocation. getCurrentPosition(). The callback function takes the position object and gets the latitude and longitude from its coords object. It then sets the latitude and longitude into the text fields:

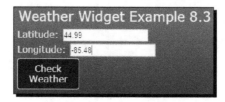

If the geolocation request failed for some reason, we get the error message from the error object and show it on the page:

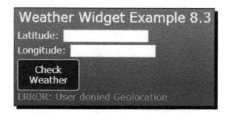

What just happened?

We used the Geolocation API to get the user's position. We extracted the latitude and longitude and displayed them in text fields on the page. We will pass this into the weather service to get the weather for their location.

Have a go hero

Create a web application that tracks the user's position using the Geolocation API. When the user's location changes, use Ajax to call the Google Static Maps API to get a map of the user's current position and update an image on the page. Open the application in your smart phone and drive around to see if it works. You can find the documentation for Google's Static Maps API at https://developers.google.com/maps/documentation/staticmaps/.

Using web services

Web services are an integral part of creating most enterprise-level web applications these days. They provide access to services that can't be accessed directly on the client side due to security restrictions. For example, you could have a web service that accesses a database to retrieve or store customer information. Web services can also provide centralized operations that can be accessed from many different applications. For example, a service that supplies weather data.

Web services can be created using any server side technology that can get a web request and return a response. It could be as simple as PHP, or as sophisticated as a service-oriented architecture such as .NET's WCF API. If you are the only one using your web service then PHP may be sufficient; if a web services is designed for public consumption, then maybe not.

Most web services provide data in either XML or JSON format. In the past, XML was the format of choice for web services. However, in recent years JSON has become very popular. Not only because more and more JavaScript applications are interacting directly with web services, but also because it is a succinct, easy-to-read, and easy-to-parse format. Many service providers are now switching over to JSON.

It is not in the scope of this book to teach you how to write web services, but we will learn how to interact with them by using a web service that provides localized weather reports.

Weather Underground

For this example we will get the weather from a real web service. We will use the service provided by Weather Underground at `http://www.wunderground.com`. To run the example code you will need a developer API key, which can be obtained for free at `http://www.wunderground.com/weather/api/`. The free developer plan allows you to call their services, but limits the number of service calls you can make per day.

Cross-site scripting and JSONP

We can call a web service using any of the jQuery Ajax methods discussed in the previous sections. There is no problem calling web services that reside in the same domain as your web page. However, calling web services that exist in another domain presents a security problem. This is known as cross-site scripting, or XSS. For example, the page at `http://mysite.com/myPage.html` can't access any content from `http://yoursite.com`.

The problem with cross-site scripting is that hackers can inject client-side scripts into a request that will allow them to run malicious code in the user's browser. So how do we get around this restriction? We can use a communication technique known as **JSONP**, which stands for **JSON with Padding**.

JSONP works due to the fact that there is a security exception for loading JavaScript files from other domains. So in order to get around the restriction of getting plain JSON formatted data, JSONP simulates a `<script>` request. The server returns the JSON data wrapped in a JavaScript function call. If we take the JSON from the previous example and put it in a JSONP response, it will look something like the following code snippet:

```
jQuery18107425144074950367_1365363393321(
{
    "location": {
        "city":"Your City"
    }
    ,"current_observation": {
        "weather":"Clear",
        "temperature_string":"38.3 F (3.5 C)",
        "wind_string":"From the WSW at 1.0 MPH Gusting to 5.0 MPH",
        "feelslike_string":"38 F (3 C)",
        "relative_humidity":"71%",
        "icon_url":"images/nt_clear.gif"
    }
}
);
```

The great thing about using jQuery to make our Ajax requests is that we don't even have to think about how JSONP works. All we need to know is that we need to use it when calling services in other domains. To tell jQuery to use JSONP we pass in a `dataType` parameter set to `"jsonp"` to the `ajax()` method.

The `ajax()` method can take in an object of name/value pairs that contains all of the parameters for making a request, including the URL. We put our `dataType` parameter in that object:

```
$.ajax({
    url: "http://otherSite/serviceCall",
    dataType : "jsonp"
});
```

Time for action – calling the weather service

Now that we have the user's location we can pass it to the Underground Weather service to get the user's current weather. We will use JSONP to call the service since the service exists in an external domain. Let's go into the `WeatherWidget` object and make a few changes.

First we need to change the constructor to take the Weather Underground API key. Since we're writing a generic widget that could go on any page on any site, the developer of the page will need to provide their key:

```
function WeatherWidget($widget, wuKey)
```

Next we will change the `getWeatherReport()` method. It now takes the coordinates of the place we want to get a weather report for. In this case it's the user's position that we got from the Geolocation API:

```
function getWeatherReport(lat, lon)
{
    var coords = lat + "," + lon;
    $.ajax({
        url: "http://api.wunderground.com/api/" + wuKey +
            "/conditions/q/" + coords + ".json",
        dataType : "jsonp"
    })
    .done(function(data) { populateWeather(data); })
    .fail(function(jqXHR, textStatus, errorThrown) {
        showError(errorThrown);
    });
}
```

We make the call to the Weather Underground service using the `ajax()` method and JSONP. The base request to the service is `http://api.wunderground.com/api/` followed by the API key. To get the current weather conditions we add `/conditions/q/` to the URL, followed by the latitude and longitude separated by a comma. Last we append `".json"` to tell the service to give us data back in JSON format. The URL ends up looking like `http://api.wunderground.com/api/xxxxxxxx/conditions/q/44.99,-85.48.json`.

The `done()` and `fail()` handlers are the same as they were in the previous example.

Now let's change the `populateWeather()` method to extract the data returned from the service:

```
function populateWeather(data)
{
    var observation = data.current_observation;

    $(".results header img", $widget).attr("src",
        observation.icon_url);
    $(".location>span",
        $widget).text(observation.display_location.full);

    $(".conditions>span").each(function(i, e)
```

```
    {
        var $span = $(this);
        var field = $span.data("field");
        $(this).text(observation[field]);
    });

    // Comply with terms of service
    $(".results footer img", $widget)
        .attr("src", observation.image.url);

    $(".loading", $widget).fadeOut(function ()
    {
        $(".results", $widget).fadeIn();
    });
}
```

This version of the `populateWeather()` method is nearly identical to the one we used for our JSON file example. The only difference is that we add an image to the footer of the widget showing the Weather Underground logo, which is part of the terms of service for using their service.

The only thing left to do is go back into the web page's main `WeatherApp` object, and change the call to `WeatherWidget` to provide the API key and location:

```
function WeatherApp()
{
    var weatherWidget =
            new WeatherWidget($("#weather-widget"), "YourApiKey"),
        version = "8.3";
```

Next we change `getCurrentWeather()`, which is called when the **Check Weather** button is clicked, to pass the user's coordinates to the widget's `update()` method:

```
function getCurrentWeather()
{
    var lat = $("#latitude").val();
    var lon = $("#longitude").val();
    if (lat && lon)
    {
        $("#weather-widget").fadeIn();
        weatherWidget.update(lat, lon);
    }
}
```

After fading in the widget, we get the coordinates from the text input fields. Then we call the widget's `update()` method, passing the coordinates to it. There you have it; the weather for the user's location is shown:

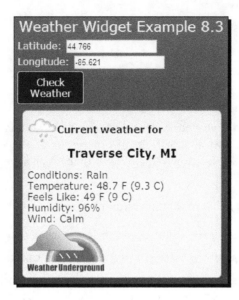

What just happened?

We changed the weather widget to use the Weather Underground service to get the current weather for the user's location, which we got from the Geolocation API. We used JSONP to call the service since it's not in the same domain as our web page.

Pop quiz

Q1. What jQuery method do you use to make an Ajax request?

1. `ajax()`
2. `get()`
3. `post()`
4. All of the above

Q2. When do you need to use JSONP to make an Ajax request?

1. When calling a web service
2. When making a request to another domain
3. When making a request to the same domain
4. When doing a POST request

Q3. What information does the Geolocation API provide?

1. The user's latitude and longitude

2. The user's country

3. The user's address

4. All of the above

Summary

In this chapter we created a weather widget that can be placed on any page. We made Ajax requests to get static XML and JSON data from the server. We learned how to find the user's location using the Geolocation API, and used that to call a web service to get localized weather data.

We covered the following concepts in this chapter:

◆   How to read XML and JSON files from the server using Ajax

◆   How to extract data from XML returned from server calls using jQuery

◆   How to get the user's current position anywhere in the world using the HTML5 Geolocation API

◆   How to interact with web services asynchronously using Ajax

◆   Using JSONP to get around the security restrictions of cross site scripting

◆   How to get the weather report for a user's current location using geolocation and a web service

In the next chapter, we will learn about creating multithreaded JavaScript applications using the Web Workers API. We will create an application that draws Mandelbrot fractals without locking up the browser.

9

Web Workers Unite

"If you want creative workers, give them enough time to play."

—John Cleese

In this chapter we will learn how to use HTML5 web workers to run background processes in another thread. We can use this to make applications with long running processes more responsive. We will draw a Mandelbrot fractal on a canvas using a web worker to generate it asynchronously without locking up the browser window.

We will learn the following topics in this chapter:

- ◆ How to make web applications more responsive by using web workers
- ◆ How to start and manage a web worker
- ◆ How to communicate with a web worker and send data back and forth
- ◆ How to draw a Mandelbrot fractal on a canvas using a web worker
- ◆ Tips for debugging web workers

Web workers

Web workers provide a way to run JavaScript code in the background on a separate thread from the main thread of a web application. Although it may seem like JavaScript is multithreaded because of its asynchronous nature, the truth is that there is only one thread. If you tie that thread up with a long running process, the web page will become unresponsive until it finishes.

In the past you could alleviate this problem by breaking long-running processes into chunks to do a little bit of the work at a time. After each chunk you would call `setTimeout()`, passing it a value of zero for the timeout. When you call `setTimeout()`, what actually happens is that an event gets put into the event queue after the amount of time specified. This allows other event already in the queue a chance to get handled until your timer event makes it to the front of the queue.

If you've ever worked with threads before you will be aware that it is easy to run into concurrency issues. One thread could be working on the same data as another thread, which could cause corrupted data, or even worse, deadlocks. Fortunately web workers don't give us much of a chance to run into concurrency issues. Web workers are not allowed to access non-thread safe components such as the DOM. They also can't access the `window`, `document`, or `parent` objects.

This thread safety does come at a price, though. Since a web worker can't access the DOM, it can't do any work that manipulates page elements. It can't directly manipulate any of the data structures from the main thread, either. At this point you might be thinking, if the web worker can't access anything then what good is it?

Well, web workers can't access data in the main thread, but they can pass data back and forth via messages. The key thing to remember, however, is that any data passed to a web worker is serialized before being sent and then de-serialized on the other end so that it is working on a copy, not the original data. The web worker can then do some processing on the data and send it back, using serialization again, to the main thread. Just remember that there will be some overhead to passing large data structures so you might still want to chunk your data and process it in smaller batches.

> Some browsers do support the ability to transfer objects without making a copy, which is great for large data structures. At this time it is only supported by a few browsers so we will not cover it here.

Spawning a web worker

The code for a web worker is defined in its own JavaScript file separate from the main application. The main thread spawns a web worker by creating a new `Worker` object giving it the path to the file:

```
var myWorker = new Worker("myWorker.js");
```

The application and the worker communicate with each other by sending messages. To receive messages we add a message event handler to the worker using `addEventListener()`:

```
myWorker.addEventListener("message", function (event) {
  alert("Message from worker: " + event.data);
}, false);
```

An `event` object gets passed as a parameter to the event handler. It has a `data` field that contains any data passed back from the worker. The `data` field can be anything that can be represented with JSON including strings, number, data objects, and arrays.

To start a worker after it has been created you send a message to it using the `postMessage()` method. It takes one optional parameter which is the data to send to the worker. In this example it's simply a string:

```
myWorker.postMessage("start");
```

Implementing a web worker

As mentioned previously, the code for the web worker is specified in a separate file. Inside a worker you also add an event listener to receive messages from the application:

```
self.addEventListener("message", function (event) {
  // Handle message
}, false);
```

Inside the worker there is a `self` keyword that references the global scope of the worker. Using the `self` keyword is optional, like using the `window` object (all global variables and functions are attached to the `window` object). We will use it here just to show the context.

The worker can send messages back to the main thread using `postMessage()`. It works exactly the same as it does in the main thread:

```
self.postMessage("started");
```

When a worker is finished it can call the `close()` method to terminate the worker. After closing, a worker it can no longer be used:

```
self.close();
```

You can also import other external JavaScript files into a worker using the `importScripts()` method. It takes the path to one or more script files:

```
importScripts("script1.js", "script2.js");
```

This works well for using the same library of code in both your main thread and the web worker.

Time for action – using a web worker

Let's create a really simple application that gets the user's name and passes it to a web worker. The web worker will return a "hello" message back to the application. The code for this section can be found in Chapter 9/example9.1.

 The web workers don't work in some browsers unless you are running them through a web server such as IIS or Apache.

First we create an application with webWorkerApp.html, webWorkerApp.css, and webWorkerApp.js files. We add a text input field to the HTML asking for the user's name and a response section to display the message from the worker:

```html
<div id="main">
    <div>
        <label for="your-name">Please enter your name: </label>
        <input type="text" id="your-name"/>
        <button id="submit">Submit</button>
    </div>
    <div id="response" class="hidden">
        The web worker says: <span></span>
    </div>
</div>
```

In webWorkerApp.js, when the user clicks on the submit button we call the executeWorker() method:

```javascript
function executeWorker()
{
    var name = $("#your-name").val();
    var worker = new Worker("helloWorker.js");
    worker.addEventListener("message", function(event) {
        $("#response").fadeIn()
            .children("span").text(event.data);
    });
    worker.postMessage(name);
}
```

First we get the name the user entered into the text field. Then we create a new Worker that has its code defined in helloWorker.js. We add a message event listener that gets a message back from the worker and puts it into the page's response section. Last but not least we send the user's name to the worker using postMessage() to start it.

Now let's create the code for our web worker in `helloWorker.js`. There we add the code to get the message from the main thread and send a message back:

```
self.addEventListener("message", function(event) {
    sayHello(event.data);
});
function sayHello(name)
{
    self.postMessage("Hello, " + name);
}
```

First we add an event listener to get the message from the application. We extract the name from the `event.data` field and pass that into the `sayHello()` function. The `sayHello()` function simply prepends "Hello" to the user's name and sends the message back to the application using `postMessage()`. Back in the main application it gets the message and displays it on the page.

What just happened?

We created a simple application that gets the user's name and passes it to a web worker. The web worker sends a message back to the application where it is displayed on the page - that's how easy it is to use web workers.

The Mandelbrot set

To demonstrate how to use web workers to do some real processing we will create an application that draws **Mandelbrot fractals**. Drawing a Mandelbrot is pretty intensive and takes a lot of processing power. If you don't run it in a separate thread, the application will become unresponsive while it's drawing.

Drawing a Mandelbrot is a relatively simple process. We will use the **escape time algorithm**. For each pixel in the image we will determine how many iterations it takes to reach a critical escape condition. The number of iterations determines the color of the pixel. If we don't reach the escape condition within a maximum number of iterations, it is considered to be inside the Mandelbrot set and we color it black.

For more information about this algorithm and the Mandelbrot set see the Wikipedia page:

```
http://en.wikipedia.org/wiki/Mandelbrot_set
```

Time for action – implementing the algorithm

Let's create a `MandelbrotGenerator` object in a new file named `mandelbrotGenerator.js`. This object will implement the algorithm that generates the Mandelbrot. The constructor takes the canvas width and height, and the bounds of the Mandelbrot:

```
function MandelbrotGenerator(canvasWidth, canvasHeight, left, top,
    right, bottom)
    {
```

Next we define the variables that the algorithm uses:

```
var scalarX = (right - left) / canvasWidth,
    scalarY = (bottom - top) / canvasHeight,
    maxIterations = 1000,
    abort = false,
    inSetColor = { r: 0x00, g: 0x00, b: 0x00 },
    colors = [ /* array of color objects */ ];
```

The `scalarX` and `scalarY` variables are used to convert the Mandelbrot coordinates to canvas coordinates. They are computed by dividing the width or height of the Mandelbrot by the width or height of the canvas. For example, while the canvas may be set to 640 by 480 pixels, the bounds of the Mandelbrot may be something like (-2, -2) for top left and (2, 2) for bottom right. In this case the Mandelbrot height and width are both 4:

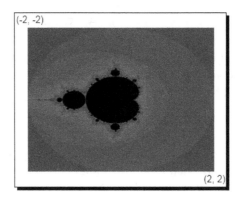

Next we set the maximum number of iterations for the algorithm to 1000. If you set it higher you will get better results but it will take longer to compute. Using 1000 provides a good middle ground between processing time and acceptable results. The `abort` variable is used to stop the algorithm. The `inSetColor` variable controls what color pixels that are in the Mandelbrot set get colored. We set it to black. Finally there is an array of colors that will get used to color pixels that aren't in the set.

Let's write those methods to convert canvas coordinates to Mandelbrot coordinates first. They simply multiply the position by the scalar and add the top or left offset:

```
function getMandelbrotX(x)
{
    return scalarX * x + left;
}
function getMandelbrotY(y)
{
    return scalarY * y + top;
}
```

Now let's define the main loop of the algorithm in a public method named `draw()`. It takes the image data from a canvas to draw on as a parameter:

```
this.draw = function(imageData)
{
    abort = false;

    for (var y = 0; y < canvasHeight; y++)
    {
        var my = getMandelbrotY(y);
        for (var x = 0; x < canvasWidth; x++)
        {
            if (abort) return;
            var mx = getMandelbrotX(x);
            var iteration = getIteration(mx, my);
            var color = getColor(iteration);
            setPixel(imageData, x, y, color);
        }
    }
};
```

In the outer loop we iterate over all of the rows of pixels in the canvas. Inside this loop we call `getMandelbrotY()`, passing in the canvas y-position and get back the corresponding y-position in the Mandelbrot.

Next we iterate over all of the pixels in the row. For each pixel we:

1. Call `getMandelbrotX()`, passing in the canvas x-position and get back the corresponding x-position in the Mandelbrot.

2. Call `getIterations()`, passing in the Mandelbrot x and y positions. This method is where it will find the number of iterations it takes to reach the escape condition.

3. Call getColor(), passing in the number of iterations. This method gets the color for the number of iterations.

4. Finally we call setPixel(), passing in the image data, x and y positions, and the color.

Let's implement the getIterations() method next. This is where we determine if the pixel is within the Mandelbrot set or not. It takes the Mandelbrot x and y positions as parameters:

```
function getIterations(x0, y0)
{
    var x = 0,
        y = 0,
        iteration = 0;
    do
    {
        iteration++;
        if (iteration >= maxIterations) return -1;
        var xtemp = x * x - y * y + x0;
        y = 2 * x * y + y0;
        x = xtemp;
    }
    while (x * x + y * y < 4);

    return iteration;
}
```

First we initialize working x and y positions to zero and the iteration counter to zero. Next we start a do-while loop. Inside the loop we increment the iteration counter and if it is more than maxIterations we return -1. This signals that the escape condition was not met and the point is inside the Mandelbrot set.

Next we compute the x and y variables for checking the escape condition. Then we check the condition to determine whether to continue with the loop. Once the escape condition has been met we return the number of iterations it took to find it.

Now we will write the getColor() method. It takes the iteration count as a parameter:

```
function getColor(iteration)
{
    if (iteration < 0) return inSetColor;
    return colors[iteration % colors.length];
}
```

If the `iteration` parameter is less than zero it means it's in the Mandelbrot set and we return the `inSetColor` object. Otherwise we look up the color object in the colors array by using the modulus operator to constrain the number of iterations to the length of the array.

Finally we will write the `setPixel()` method. It takes the image data, canvas x and y positions, and the color:

```
function setPixel(imageData, x, y, color)
{
    var d = imageData.data;
    var index = 4 * (canvasWidth * y + x);
    d[index] = color.r;
    d[index + 1] = color.g;
    d[index + 2] = color.b;
    d[index + 3] = 255; // opacity
}
```

This should look very familiar from *Chapter 5, Not So Blank Canvas*, where we learned how to manipulate image data. First we find the index of the pixel in the image data array. Then we set each of the color channels from the `color` object and set the opacity to the maximum value of `255`.

What just happened?

We implemented the algorithm to draw a Mandelbrot to a canvas's image data. Each pixel is set to either black if it's in the Mandelbrot set or some color depending on how many iterations it took to find the escape condition.

Creating a Mandelbrot application

Now that we have the algorithm implemented let's create an application that uses it to draw a Mandelbrot on the page. We will start off drawing it without a web worker to show how the process makes the web page unresponsive. Then we will use a web worker to draw the Mandelbrot in the background to see the difference.

Time for action – creating a Mandelbrot application

Let's start off by creating a new application with `mandelbrot.html`, `mandelbrot.css`, and `mandelbrot.js` files. We also include `mandelbrotGenerator.js` we created previously for the application. You can find the code for this section in `Chapter 9/example9.2`.

In the HTML file we add a `<canvas>` element to the HTML to draw the Mandelbrot on and set the size to 640 by 480:

```
<canvas width="640" height="480"></canvas>
```

We also add three buttons with pre-set Mandelbrot bounds defined as arrays in JSON format in the `data-settings` custom data attribute:

```
<button class="draw"
    data-settings="[-2, -2, 2, 2]">Draw Full</button>
<button class="draw"
    data-settings="[-0.225, -0.816, -0.197, -0.788]">Preset 1
</button>
<button class="draw"
    data-settings="[-1.18788, -0.304, -1.18728, -0.302]">Preset 2

</button>
```

Now let's go into the JavaScript file and add the code to call the Mandelbrot generator. Here we define variables to hold references to the canvas and its context:

```
function MandelbrotApp()
{
    var version = "9.2",
        canvas = $("canvas")[0],
        context = canvas.getContext("2d");
```

Next we add a `drawMandelbrot()` method that will get called when one of the buttons is clicked. It takes the bounds of the Mandelbrot to draw as parameters:

```
function drawMandelbrot(left, top, right, bottom)
{
    setStatus("Drawing...");
    var imageData =
        context.getImageData(0, 0, canvas.width, canvas.height);
    var generator = new MandelbrotGenerator(canvas.width, canvas.
height,
        left, top, right, bottom);
    generator.draw(imageData);
    context.putImageData(imageData, 0, 0)
    setStatus("Finished.");
}
```

First we display a status of **Drawing...** in the status bar. Then we get the image data for the entire canvas. Next we create a new instance of the `MandelbrotGenerator` object, passing in the canvas and bounds settings. Then we call its `draw()` method passing, in the image data. When it has finished we draw the image data back to the canvas and set the status to **Finished**.

The last thing we need to do is update the application's `start()` method:

```
this.start = function()
{
    $("#app header").append(version);

    $("button.draw").click(function() {
        var data = $(this).data("settings");
        drawMandelbrot(data[0], data[1], data[2], data[3]);
    });

    setStatus("ready");
};
```

Here we add one click event handler for all of the buttons. When a button is clicked on we get the `settings` custom data attribute, which is an array, and pass the values into `drawMandelbrot()` to draw it.

That's it- let's open it in the browser and take a look. Depending on the browser you are using (some are a lot faster than others) and the speed of your system, the Mandelbrot should take long enough to draw that you notice the page has become unresponsive. If you try to click one of the other buttons nothing will happen. Also notice that although we call `setStatus("Drawing...")` you never see the status actually change. That's because the drawing algorithm takes over before the runtime gets a chance to update the text on the page:

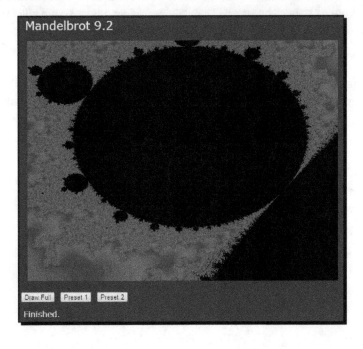

What just happened?

We created an application to draw Mandelbrot sets using the drawing algorithm we created in the previous section. It doesn't use a web worker yet, so the page becomes unresponsive while it's drawing.

Time for action – Mandelbrot using a web worker

Now we will implement the same thing except this time we will use a web worker to offload the processing onto another thread. This will free up the main thread to handle page updates and user interaction. You can find the source code for this section in Chapter 9/example9.3.

Let's go into the HTML and add a checkbox where we can select whether to use web workers or not. This will make it easier to compare results in the browser:

```
<input type="checkbox" id="use-worker" checked />
<label for="use-worker">Use web worker</label>
```

We'll also add a stop button. There was no way to stop before without web workers because the UI was locked up, but now we will be able to implement it:

```
<button id="stop">Stop Drawing</button>
```

Now let's go ahead and create our web worker in a new file named mandelbrotWorker. js. Our worker needs to use the MandelbrotGenerator object so we will import that script into the worker:

```
importScripts("mandelbrotGenerator.js");
```

Now let's define our message event handler for the worker. Upon receiving a message with the data necessary to draw the Mandelbrot, the worker will start generating it:

```
self.addEventListener("message", function(e)
{
    var data = e.data;
    var generator = new MandelbrotGenerator(data.width, data.height,
        data.left, data.top, data.right, data.bottom);
    generator.draw(data.imageData);
    self.postMessage(data.imageData);
    self.close();
});
```

First we create a new instance of `MandelbrotGenerator`, passing in the values we got from the main application thread including the canvas width and height and the Mandelbrot bounds. Then we call the generator's `draw()` method, passing in the image data which is also included in the message. After the generator is done, we pass the image data with the Mandelbrot drawn into back to the main thread by calling `postMessage()` with the image data as the parameter. Lastly, we call `close()` to terminate the worker.

That's it for the worker. Let's go back to our main application object, `MandelbrotApp` and add code to start the web worker when one of the buttons is clicked.

Back in `mandelbrot.js`, we need to add a global variable to the application object named worker that will hold a reference to the web worker. Then we rewrite `drawMandelbrot()` to add some new code to start the worker:

```
function drawMandelbrot(left, top, right, bottom)
{
    if (worker) return;

    context.clearRect(0, 0, canvas.width, canvas.height);
    setStatus("Drawing...");

    var useWorker = $("#use-worker").is(":checked");
    if (useWorker)
    {
        startWorker(left, top, right, bottom);
    }
    else
    {
        /* Draw without worker */
    }
}
```

First we check if the `worker` variable is set. If so the worker is already running and there's no need to continue. Then we clear the canvas and set the status. Next we check if the **Use worker** checkbox is checked. If so, we call `startWorker()`, passing in the Mandelbrot bounds parameters. The `startWorker()` method is where we create the web worker and start it:

```
function startWorker(left, top, right, bottom)
{
    worker = new Worker("mandelbrotWorker.js");
    worker.addEventListener("message", function(e)
    {
        context.putImageData(e.data, 0, 0)
        worker = null;
```

```
        setStatus("Finished.");
    );

    var imageData =
        context.getImageData(0, 0, canvas.width, canvas.height);
    worker.postMessage({
        imageData: imageData,
        width: canvas.width,
        height: canvas.height,
        left: left,
        top: top,
        right: right,
        bottom: bottom
    });
}
```

First we create a new `Worker`, passing into it the path to `mandelbrotWorker.js`. Then we add a message event handler to the worker which will get called when it is done. It takes the image data it got back from the worker and draws it to the canvas.

Next we start the worker. First we get the image data from the canvas's context. Then we put the image data, the canvas width and height, and the Mandelbrot bounds into an object that we pass to the worker by calling `postMessage()`.

There's one thing left to do. We need to implement the stop button. Let's write a `stopWorker()` method that will be called when the stop button is clicked:

```
function stopWorker()
{
    if (worker)
    {
        worker.terminate();
        worker = null;
        setStatus("Stopped.");
    }
}
```

First we check if the worker is running by checking if the `worker` variable is set. If so we call the worker's `terminate()` method to stop the worker. Calling `terminate()` is equivalent to calling `self.close()` from inside the worker.

What just happened?

We implemented a web worker that can draw the Mandelbrot from a background thread. This allows the user to continue to interact with the page while the Mandelbrot is drawing. We demonstrated this by adding a stop button that can stop the drawing process. You will also notice that the **Drawing...** status message now gets displayed while the fractal is being drawn.

Have a go hero

One problem with our Mandelbrot application is that we are serializing and transferring the entire canvas's image data to the web worker and back. In our example that is 640 * 480 * 4 bytes, or 1,228,800 bytes. That's 1.2 GB! See if you can come up with a way to chunk up the drawing of the Mandelbrot into smaller pieces. If you want to see how I did it look at Chapter 9/example9.4.

Debugging web workers

Debugging web workers can be difficult. You don't have access to the `window` object so you can't call `alert()` to display a message or `console.log()` to write out to the browser's JavaScript console. You can't write out a message to the DOM either. You can't even attach a debugger and step through the code. So what's a poor developer to do?

One thing you can do is add an error listener to the worker, so you get notified of any errors inside the worker's thread:

```
worker.addEventListener("error", function(e)
{
    alert("Error in worker: " + e.filename + ", line:" + e.lineno + ",
" + e.message);
});
```

The event object passed into the error handler contains the `filename`, `lineno`, and `message` fields. From those you can tell exactly where an error happened.

But what if you aren't getting an error, things just aren't working right? First of all, I recommend that you keep the code that does all of the processing for your worker in a separate file, like we did in `mandelbrotGenerator.js`. This allows you to run the code from your main thread as well as a worker. If you need to debug it you can run it directly from the application and debug as you normally would.

One debugging trick you can use is to define a `console` object in your web worker that sends messages back to the main thread where they can be logged using the window's console:

```
var console = {
    log: function(msg)
    {
        self.postMessage({
            type: "log",
            message: msg
        });
    }
};
```

In your application, you then listen for the message and log it:

```
worker.addEventListener("message", function(e)
{
    if (e.data.type == "log")
    {
        console.log(e.data.message);
    }
});
```

Pop quiz

Q1. How do you send data to a web worker?

1. You can't send data to a worker.
2. Using the `postMessage()` method.
3. Using the `sendData()` method.
4. Using the `sendMessage()` method.

Q2. Which resource in the main thread does a web worker have access to?

1. The DOM.
2. The `window` object.
3. The `document` object.
4. None of the above.

Summary

In this chapter we created an application to draw Mandelbrot fractals to learn how to use HTML web workers to execute long running processes in a background thread. This allowed the browser to remain responsive and accept user input while generating the image.

We covered the following concepts in this chapter:

- How to use web workers to make web applications more responsive
- How to create a web worker and start it
- How to send messages and data between the main thread and the web worker
- How to draw a Mandelbrot using a web worker
- How to catch errors thrown from a web worker
- How to debug web workers

In the next and final chapter we will learn how to prepare a web application for release by combining and compressing its JavaScript files. This will give the application a lighter network footprint. In addition we will see how to use the HTML5 Application Cache to cache an application so it will run even when the user is offline.

10
Releasing an App into the Wild

"The Internet is a wild land with its own games, languages, and gestures through which we are starting to share common feelings."

– Ai Weiwei

In this chapter we will learn how to prepare a web application for release. First we will discuss how to compress and combine JavaScript files for faster download times. Then we will look at how to use the HTML5 Application Cache interface to make your applications available offline.

In this chapter we will learn:

- How to combine and compress JavaScript files
- How to create a command-line script to prepare an application for release
- How to use the HTML5 Application Cache API to make a page and its resources available offline
- How to create a cache manifest file to determine what resources get cached
- How to determine when an application's cache has been updated

Combining and compressing JavaScript

In the past, the conventional wisdom among JavaScript developers was that you should write all of your code in one file, because downloading multiple script files causes a lot of unnecessary network traffic and slows down the load time. While reducing the number of files to download is indeed better, writing all of your code in one file is difficult to read and maintain. We don't write code like that in other languages, so why should we do it in JavaScript?

Fortunately there is a solution to this problem: the JavaScript compressor. A compressor takes all of the JavaScript source files for an application, combines them into one file, and compresses them by renaming local variables to the smallest name possible, removing white space and comments. We get all of the benefits of using multiple source code files for development, plus all of the benefits of a single JavaScript file when releasing an application. You can think of it as compiling your source code into a compact executable package.

There are a number of JavaScript compressors available out there. You can find many of them online. The problem with those is that you have to copy your source code and paste it into a web form, then copy it back out into a file. That doesn't work too well for large applications. I suggest you use one of the compression applications that can be run from a command prompt, such as Yahoo's YUI Compressor or Google's Closure Compiler:

- `https://developers.google.com/closure/`
- `http://yui.github.io/yuicompressor/`

YUI and Closure are both easy to use and work extremely well. They both provide warnings about bad code (but not the same warnings). Both are written in Java and therefore require that you have the Java Runtime installed. I can't say one is better than the other. The only reason I would choose YUI would be if I also want to compress CSS, as Closure doesn't support it.

Time for action – creating a release script

The easiest way to prepare your JavaScript for release is to create a script that can be run from the command line. In this example we will use the YUI Compressor, but it works almost identically for Closure. The only difference is the command-line parameters. In this example we create a command-line script that can be run from the Windows command line, that will take the Piano Hero application we wrote in *Chapter 7, Piano Hero*, and package it up for release. You can find the code for this section in `Chapter 10/example10.1`.

Before we start, we need to define a folder structure for the application. I like to create a base folder for the application that contains a `src` folder and a `release` folder. The base folder contains the command-line batch script. The `src` folder contains all of the source code and resources. The `release` folder will contain the compressed JavaScript file and all other resources necessary to run the application:

Now let's create our batch script file and name it `release.bat`. The first thing we need to tell YUI is what files to compress. There are a couple of ways to do this. We can either concatenate all of our JavaScript files into one file and then reference that one file, or pass in a list of all the individual files. The method you use depends on your needs.

If you need the files to be processed in a certain order, or you don't have a lot of files, then you can specify them individually as parameters. If you have a lot of files in your application and you're not worried about order, then it's probably easiest to just concatenate them into one file. For this example, we will use the `type` command to concatenate all JavaScript files into one file named `pianoHero.collated.js`:

```
type src\*.js > pianoHero.collated.js
```

We use the `type` command to find all `.js` files in the `src` folder and write them out to a file named `pianoHero.collated.js`. Note this does not include the files in the `lib` folder. I like to keep them separate, but you can certainly include any external libraries if you prefer (and if their license permits it). Now we will execute the compressor passing in the collated JavaScript file:

```
java -jar ..\yui\yuicompressor-2.4.6.jar --type js -o
    release\pianoHero.min.js pianoHero.collated.js
```

We start the Java runtime telling it where to find the YUI Compressor's JAR file. We pass in a file type parameter of `js` since we are compressing JavaScript (YUI can also compress CSS). The `-o` parameter tells it where to write the output to. The last is the JavaScript file (or files if more than one) we want to compress.

Now we have a `pianoHero.min.js` file in the `release` folder. We still need to copy all of the other resources to the `release` folder including the HTML and CSS files, the jQuery library, and the audio files:

```
xcopy /Y src\*.html release
xcopy /Y src\*.css release
xcopy /Y /S /I src\lib release\lib
xcopy /Y /S /I src\audio release\audio
```

We use the `xcopy` command to copy `pianoHero.html`, `pianoHero.css`, everything in the `lib` folder, and everything in the `audio` folder to the `release` folder. At this point we have everything we need in the `release` folder to run the application.

There's one last thing to do. We need to remove the obsolete `<script>` elements in the HTML file and replace them with one that points to our compressed JavaScript file. This part isn't easy to automate, so we need to crack the file open and do this manually:

```
<head>
    <title>Piano Hero</title>
    <link href="pianoHero.css" rel="StyleSheet" />
```

```
        <script src="lib/jquery-1.8.1.min.js"></script>
        <script src="pianoHero.min.js"></script>
    </head>
```

That's it. Now open the application in your browser and do a smoke test to make sure everything still works the way you expect it and then ship it!

What just happened?

We created a Windows command-line script to combine all of our JavaScript source files into one and compress it using the YUI Compressor. We also copied all of the resources necessary to run the application to the `release` folder. Lastly, we changed the script reference to the compressed JavaScript file.

Have a go hero

The YUI Compressor also minifies CSS. Add code to the release script to compress the CSS file.

HTML5 Application Cache

The HTML5 Application Cache API provides a mechanism for caching the files and resources used by a web page. Once cached, it's as if the user downloaded and installed your application on their device. This allows the application to be used offline when the user is not connected to the Internet.

 Browsers may limit the amount of data that can be cached. Some browsers limit it to 5 MB.

The key to getting your application cached is the cache manifest file. This file is a simple text file that contains information about what resources should be cached. It is referenced by the `manifest` attribute on the `<html>` element of your web page:

```
<html manifest="myapp.appcache">
```

Inside the manifest file, you can specify the resources to cache or not cache. The file can have three sections:

- ◆ CACHE: This is the default section and lists the files to be cached. Declaring this section header is optional. Wildcards are not allowed in URIs.

- ◆ NETWORK: This section lists the files that require a network connection. Requests for these files bypass the cache. Wildcards are allowed.

◆ FALLBACK: This section lists fallback files if a resource is not available offline. Each entry contains the URI of the original file and the URI of the fallback file. Wildcards are allowed. Both URIs must be relative and from the same domain as the application.

 The cache manifest file can have any file extension, but it must be delivered with a MIME type of text/cache-manifest. You may need to associate the extension you use with this MIME type in your web server.

One important thing to note is that once the files for an application are cached only those versions of the files will be used, even if they change on the server. There are only two ways that the resources in the application cache can be updated:

◆ When the manifest file changes

◆ When the user clears the browser's data storage for your application

I recommend keeping the cache manifest file out of the same folder as your HTML file while developing your application. You don't want files cached while you are writing code. Put it in the base folder of your application along with your release script and copy it to the release folder in your script.

Whether you cache your application or not depends on the nature of your application. If it heavily depends upon Ajax calls to the server to work then making it available offline would be pointless. However, if you can write your application so that it stores data locally while offline, then it might be worthwhile. You should determine if the overhead of maintaining a cache manifest provides a benefit to your application.

Time for action – creating a cache manifest

Let's create a simple application from our template to demonstrate how to use the cache manifest. It has HTML, CSS, and JavaScript files, and a couple of images in an image folder. You can find the source code for this example in Chapter 10/example10.2.

Now let's create a cache manifest file named app.appcache:

```
CACHE MANIFEST
# v10.2.01
```

The manifest file must always begin with CACHE MANIFEST on the first line. On the second line we have a comment. Lines that start with a hash mark (#) are comments. It's recommended that you have some type of version identifier or the release date in the comments of your manifest file. As noted previously, the only way to cause your application to be reloaded into the cache is to change the manifest file. Each time you release a new version you will need to update this version identifier.

Next, we add the files that we want cached. You can add the CACHE section header if you like, but it's not required:

```
CACHE:
app.html
app.css
app.js
lib/jquery-1.8.1.min.js
```

Unfortunately wildcards are not allowed in this section, so you will need to explicitly list each file. For some applications, like Piano Hero with all of its audio files, that could be a lot of typing!

Next let's define the NETWORK section. Right about now you may be thinking, what's the point of this section? We already listed all of the files we want to be cached. So why the need to list files that you don't want to be cached? The reason is that once cached, your application will only get files from the cache, even when online. If you want to use non-cached resources in your application you will need to include them in this section.

For example, let's say that we have a site tracking image on our page to keep track of page hits. If we don't add it to the NETWORK section, the request for it will never get to the server, even when the user is online. For the sake of this example we will use a static image file. In practice this would be PHP or some other server-side request handler that returns an image:

```
NETWORK:
images/tracker.png
```

Now let's define the FALLBACK section. Say we want to display an image in our application that lets the user know if they are online or offline. This is where we specify a fallback from an online to an offline image:

```
FALLBACK:
online.png offline.png
```

That's it for our manifest file. Now open the application in the browser so it gets cached. Then go into the JavaScript file and change the value of the version variable in the application object. Now refresh the page; nothing should change. Next go into the manifest file and change the version and refresh again. It still didn't change. What happened?

Remember how I said earlier that when the manifest file changes, it causes the application to be reloaded? While this is true, the manifest file does not get checked for changes until after the page has been loaded from the cache. Therefore the user would need to reload the page twice to get the updated version. Fortunately there is a way we can detect in JavaScript when the manifest file has changed and give the user a message that a newer version is available.

Let's add a JavaScript method called checkIfUpdateAvailable() to check when the cache has been updated:

```
function checkIfUpdateAvailable()
{
    window.applicationCache.addEventListener('updateready',
    function(e)
    {
        setStatus("A newer version is available. Reload the page to
            update.");
    });
}
```

First we add an updateready event listener to the applicationCache object. This gets fired after the browser finds that the manifest file has changed and has downloaded the updated resources. When we receive a notification that the cache has been updated, we display a message telling the user to reload the page. Now all we have to do is add a call to this method in the start() method of our application and we are ready to go.

Now go update the version number in the application and the manifest file and refresh the page. You should see the update message displayed. Refresh the page again and you will see that the version has changed:

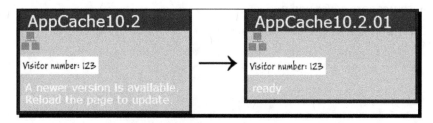

Lastly, let's check our fallback. Disconnect your Internet connection and reload the page. You should see that the offline image is shown instead of online. Also notice that it couldn't load the tracking image because we marked it as a non-cached resource:

What just happened?

We learned how to use the HTML Application Cache to cache a web application. We used a manifest file to define resources that should be cached, a resource that was not cached, and another with a fallback when the application is offline. We also learned how to programmatically check when the cache has been updated.

Pop quiz

Q1. What does a JavaScript compressor *not* do?

1. Zip your code up into a compressed file
2. Combine your JavaScript files into one file
3. Remove all white space and comments from JavaScript files
4. Rename local variables to the smallest name possible

Q2. When are resources updated in the application cache?

1. When a file changes on the server
2. When the manifest file changes
3. Resources are never updated
4. Every time the user starts the application

Summary

In this chapter we learned how to take our finished applications and prepare them for release to the world. We used a JavaScript compressor to combine and compress all of our JavaScript files into one compact file. Then we used the Application Cache API to make an application available offline.

We covered the following concepts in this chapter:

- How to combine and compress JavaScript files using the YUI Compressor
- How to create a command-line script that packages up our applications and gets them ready for release
- How to use the Application Cache API to cache an application and make it available offline
- How to create a cache manifest file and define cached, non-cached, and fallback files
- How to programmatically check when the manifest file has changed and alert the user that an update is available

There you have it. We have covered HTML5 web application development from creating a starting template to preparing your application for release. Now go out there and start writing your own HTML5 web applications. I look forward to seeing how you use HTML5 to create the next big thing.

Pop Quiz Answers

Chapter 1, The Task at Hand

Pop quiz

Q1	4
Q2	4

Chapter 2, Let's Get Stylish

Pop quiz

Q1	4
Q2	1

Chapter 3, The Devil is in the details

Pop quiz

Q1	2
Q2	4

Chapter 4, A Blank Canvas

Pop quiz

Q1	3
Q2	2

Chapter 5, Not So Blank Canvas

Pop quiz

Q1	1
	Touch events can have any number of points associated with them stored in the `touches` array
Q2	3
	Four bytes per pixel representing red, green, blue, and alpha values

Chapter 6, Piano Man

Pop quiz

Q1	4
Q2	2

Chapter 7, Piano Hero

Pop quiz

Q1	3
Q2	1

Chapter 8, A Change in the Weather

Q1	4
Q2	2
Q3	1

Chapter 9, Web Workers Unite

Q1	2
Q2	4

Chapter 10, Releasing an App into the Wild

Q1	1
Q2	2

Index

Thank you for buying
HTML5 Web Application Development By
Example Beginner's Guide

About Packt Publishing

Packt, pronounced 'packed', published its first book "Mastering phpMyAdmin for Effective MySQL Management" in April 2004 and subsequently continued to specialize in publishing highly focused books on specific technologies and solutions.

Our books and publications share the experiences of your fellow IT professionals in adapting and customizing today's systems, applications, and frameworks. Our solution-based books give you the knowledge and power to customize the software and technologies you're using to get the job done. Packt books are more specific and less general than the IT books you have seen in the past. Our unique business model allows us to bring you more focused information, giving you more of what you need to know, and less of what you don't.

Packt is a modern, yet unique publishing company, which focuses on producing quality, cutting-edge books for communities of developers, administrators, and newbies alike. For more information, please visit our website: www.PacktPub.com.

Writing for Packt

We welcome all inquiries from people who are interested in authoring. Book proposals should be sent to author@packtpub.com. If your book idea is still at an early stage and you would like to discuss it first before writing a formal book proposal, contact us; one of our commissioning editors will get in touch with you.

We're not just looking for published authors; if you have strong technical skills but no writing experience, our experienced editors can help you develop a writing career, or simply get some additional reward for your expertise.

Responsive Web Design with HTML5 and CSS3

ISBN: 978-1-84969-318-9   Paperback: 324 pages

Learn responsive design using HTML5 and CSS3 to adapt websites to any browser or screen size

1. Everything needed to code websites in HTML5 and CSS3 that are responsive to every device or screen size

2. Learn the main new features of HTML5 and use CSS3's stunning new capabilities including animations, transitions and transformations

3. Real world examples show how to progressively enhance a responsive design while providing fall backs for older browsers

HTML5 iPhone Web Application Development

ISBN: 978-1-84969-102-4   Paperback: 338 pages

An introduction to web application development for mobile within the iOS Safari browser

1. Simple and complex problems will be covered with examples and resources that backup the approach and technique.

2. Real world solutions that are broken down for multiple target audiences; from beginner developers to technical architects.

3. Learn to build true web applications using the latest industry standards for iOS Safari.

HTML5 Boilerplate Web Development

ISBN: 978-1-84951-850-5   Paperback: 174 pages

Master Web Development with a robust set of templates to get your projects done quickly and effectively

1. Master HTML5 Boilerplate as starting templates for future projects

2. Learn how to optimize your workflow with HTML5 Boilerplate templates and set up servers optimized for performance

3. Learn to feature-detect and serve appropriate styles and scripts across browser types

HTML5 Canvas Cookbook

ISBN: 978-1-84969-136-9   Paperback: 348 pages

Over 80 recipes to revolutionize the web experience with HTML5 Canvas

1. The quickest way to get up to speed with HTML5 Canvas application and game development

2. Create stunning 3D visualizations and games without Flash

3. Written in a modern, unobtrusive, and objected oriented JavaScript style so that the code can be reused in your own applications.

Please check **www.PacktPub.com** for information on our titles

www.ingramcontent.com/pod-product-compliance
Lightning Source LLC
LaVergne TN
LVHW062309060326
832902LV00013B/2133